THE SEVENTH COMMANDMENT

THE SEVENTH COMMANDMENT

SARAH SHEARS

Author of
Tapioca for Tea
Gather No Moss

PAUL ELEK LONDON

In memory of my dear love

ISBN.0.236 15485 0

Published in Great Britain by

ELEK BOOKS LIMITED

54-58 Caledonian Road, London N1 9RN

Printed by

Weatherby Woolnough Limited

Sanders Road, Wellingborough, Northants. NN8 4BX

CONTENTS

1

The Hostel

'Can you remember what you said to me that first evening when I arrived at your door?' Paul asked, as we walked back hand-in-hand down the cinder track to the ugly sprawling buildings of the hostel.

'Not a word,' I confessed.

'You said, "Welcome home, Paul!" '

'Did I?'

'It was the nicest thing anyone said to me in years, and just about the lousiest place on earth to call home, I had reckoned, when I first set eyes on it. But you disagreed with that, I remember. How come you felt that way about a communal hostel after only a week?'

'Because of the "boys". On my own I may have seen it differently, but it's people who matter to me, and they were waiting to be looked after, all twenty-nine of them!' I chuckled at the memory.

'Do I have to share you with twenty-nine other guys?' he demanded.

'You do,' I told him firmly.

He grinned with unabashed candour. 'Well, it's nice to know I'm top priority, my sweet. I mean, you wouldn't want to sleep with any of the others, would you?'

'Don't be so sure. I like variety. It's the spice of life!' I retorted.

It hadn't occurred to Paul that a woman of thirty-four would still be a virgin – untouched, innocent of sex. To turn the key in the lock of my own little room on Block Eight, and to fold me in his arms was not enough for him at the end of the day. For me, in those early days as a housekeeper, exhausted physically with cleaning and changing beds, and exhausted emotionally, I would have been content to lie in his arms, to be spoiled a little, for it was a long time since I had known any spoiling, or heard the word 'darling' on a man's lips.

Paul had no shyness, and no embarrassment. Every function of the human body was as natural as breathing. As the only boy, in a family of six sisters, and his mother's adored 'Benjamin', he had watched the girls sponging themselves in ice-cold water, Summer and Winter, and adorning themselves in pretty finery, to meet their lovers. It was natural – everything was natural, he declared, and was puzzled by my modesty.

'How come you're so scared to let me see you naked?'

'Not even my own sister or brothers have ever seen me naked,' I reminded him.

'Nobody? – not ever?'

'Only my mother, and the doctors and nurses in hospital.'

He kissed me then with a tenderness I had not known he possessed, for he kept it apart, for the child – the little girl who was six years old in that Summer of 1942, and living with her mother and maternal grand-parents in Ireland, till the end of the war.

It would always be a love of the senses, not the intellect. His brilliant mind had no part in it, just as the child had no part in it. I did not realize, till later, that a man could segregate his private and public life so completely. But while Paul was confident and boastful of our attachment, I was consumed with doubt and sadness that dimmed the spontaneous gaiety of my companion so often in that first Summer together. It was inevitable that such moments should arise in a courtship like ours, and for all Paul's platitudes and promises he could not convince me it was harming nobody. I suppose, at that time, I was essentially an honest person, and to be in love with another woman's husband seemed not only dishonest, but wicked. It was breaking the Seventh Commandment, and, to me, the Commandments were the laws of God, not to be compared with man-made laws. It was the beginning of an era of lying and pretence to my family and friends. I could only be honest with myself, for I knew exactly what I was doing, and had the unhappy result of sad, illicit love affairs all around me – deserted wives, unmarried mothers, pregnant girls sent home in disgrace.

For Paul, there was no past and no future, only the present. He had little curiosity about me as a person, but accepted me as he found me – a simple soul, in a faded cotton frock! My one small talent, as a writer of stories and verse, and the fascination of words I had known since early childhood, amused and surprised him, but he was not creative, or imaginative, so could not understand its importance. Neither could he see that an insatiable curiosity of life and people gave me the material I needed as a writer.

My curiosity about my lover was too avid and he answered all my questions briefly and impatiently. I had yet to learn there was a time and a place to question a man on any subject under the sun without eruption, but I was still a novice!

I wanted to know about his family, his early environment, his work, his ambitions, his child and, in particular, his wife.

'What is her name?'

'Jacqueline.'

'What is she like?'

'Very beautiful.'

'Does she know about me?'

'Certainly not!'

'Would she come here if she knew about us?'

'She might, but not because she cared. We had separated long before I met you.'

'Does the child know?'

'Certainly not!'

'You haven't told me her name.'

'Rosalinde.'

'Is she pretty?'

'Very pretty.'

'Like her mother?'

'Yes, but she has my eyes.'

'Does she go to school in Ireland?'

'Yes, to a Convent in Londonderry.'

'Oh, is she a Catholic?'

'Yes, we are all Catholics.'

'You didn't tell me.'

'You didn't ask. What difference does it make?'

I shook my head sadly, and he pulled me on to his knees.

'Sweetheart, I love you. I need you. Isn't that enough?'

'Yes.'

But I knew already that Paul would never marry me, for

Catholics did not recognize divorce.

* * * * *

As an executive at the nearby aircraft factory, Paul had expected decent accommodation in a local hotel or private lodgings. It was unavailable, and a temporary billet at the hostel was the only alternative. To say he was surprised would be too mild a statement, for Paul Taylor was downright disgusted! I heard about it from Nellie, a housemaid colleague, who had a niece in Reception. By the time I saw him, striding purposefully towards Block Eight that Saturday evening in May, he had, to quote Nellie, 'blown his top' and cooled down sufficiently to wear a beaming smile. But his temper, I soon discovered, was a short, sudden storm, quickly over, with no sulks, and he always apologized.

Enthusiasm was another quality I admired, and Paul had it in abundance. The more general attitude, I had noticed, was one of disgruntled disinterest, and 'I couldn't care less' was all too common an expression. He and I, in our widely different spheres as Personnel Manager and hostel housemaid, had this in common, and it was easily recognized by our contemporaries, for enthusiasm is obvious and cannot be ignored. I was already attacked for it before Paul arrived, and, in the opinion of one of my night workers on the Block, was 'so darn enthusiastic, he was nearly gassed by the smell of disinfectant'.

Paul Taylor and his room-mate the Major were model residents, making their beds, emptying the cocoa-lid ash-tray, and leaving the room so clean and tidy that I was moved to tears of gratitude after coping with the rest. But according to Nellie, my 'boys' were angels compared to her 'girls'. 'Powder all over the place, their smalls dripping in the bathrooms, and clothes chucked on the floor!' she told me, indignantly. 'But you want to watch out with that new chap on your Block, for you're getting yourself talked about,' she cautioned one morning, over her third cup of tea. 'Yanks are all the same, Sarah. Bigheads! Why can't he keep it quiet that you and him is going together? You mark my words if that new Welfare Officer isn't on your track soon for breaking the rules.'

'What rules, Nellie?' I asked, with a guilty blush.

'Men visiting women in their rooms late at night, and vicey-verser – taking meals out of the canteen – and using an electric fire to make coffee, when it's supposed to be took away till October.'

I choked on the bread and margarine, and walked slowly back to Block Eight that morning. So the 'grape-vine' had spies watching our every movement? Only to us was our love rather special and important. To the management and the gossips, we were smeared with the same tarnish as the rest of the offenders. I was shocked and dismayed, but Paul was merely amused, and enjoyed the publicity that his unorthodox behaviour had aroused. The Manager, over a friendly drink in his private office, suggested he should move to an hotel at Bath, where a room had been made available, and transport could be arranged to and from the factory.

'No, thanks. I like it here. It suits me fine,' Paul decided.

'But are you being fair to Sarah Shears?' The question annoyed Paul.

'That's my business.'

'Agreed, but you could make less noise about it. Some seem to manage to keep it dark.'

'Why should I?'

'As an educated man, you could set a better example. If you stay here, Taylor, you must abide by the rules of the place, and not expect preferential treatment.'

'Oh, go to hell!' Paul exploded, walking out of the office. He came back to repeat every word of the conversation to me, with the same disarming grin that transformed a middle-aged executive into the boy he used to be.

Coffee from the blackmarket was brewing again in the big enamel jug, and Paul, in shirtsleeves, was frying eggs in a pan on the electric fire in my bedroom, one evening in July, when a tap on the door startled me.

'Come in!' yelled Paul, quite unabashed by callers at any hour of the day or night.

The visitor I had been expecting for so long stepped inside – a tall, sparse figure in a tailored costume, hat and gloves.

'Good evening, Mr Taylor. Quite domesticated, I see! Good evening, Sarah.'

'Good evening, Miss Jackson,' I mumbled. 'Won't you sit down?'

I pushed the chair towards her, and she sat down, still gaping at Paul.

'You seem a little surprised, Ma'am. Did you expect to find us in bed?' he asked.

Now the visitor's face had flushed, and her forced gaiety turned to annoyance. 'I was under the impression that all electric fires were confiscated on the first of May, and that eggs and coffee were strictly rationed.'

'That is correct,' he agreed – taking my hand with an encouraging smile.

'So you consider it amusing to break all the rules in the hostel?'

'Very amusing, Ma'am!' he chuckled.

For a moment she seemed a little uncertain how to deal with this particular rebel, then quickly rallied, and asked frigidly, 'Is the canteen food not sufficient?'

'It's lousy!'

'Where do you obtain all these extras?' She waved a hand at the coffee she refused to sample, and the eggs hardening in the pan.

'That's my business.' He frowned, and covered the eggs with a plate, impatient to start on his supper.

I had taken several slices of bread and margarine from the canteen at staff tea-break, and smuggled them out in my overall pockets. The guilt I felt was so much in excess of the crime.

With no apology from Paul, and no sign of repentance, Miss Jackson got ready to go. 'I am afraid you leave me no alternative, Mr Taylor, but to report you both to the London Management Committee,' she informed him importantly. 'As for you, Sarah, you must abide by the rules or face a possible transfer.'

I nodded mutely.

'As a *domestic*, of course, you hardly qualify for the same privileges as Mr Taylor,' she reminded me.

Paul's amusement turned to anger in a split second. He pushed past her and threw open the door.

'Get out!' he said, his eyes blazing. When he had closed the door, and enfolded me in his arms, I knew we should have to fight for the privilege to be together, and that in future I must find courage and determination to equal Paul's.

But I wept on his shoulder for the wife I longed to be, and could never be, while the forces of law and order were ranged against us. . .

I was the first to be summoned to the 'Court of Enquiry', and in the intervening week, suffered a bad attack of migraine, for my nerves were ragged, and my mind tortured with the possibility of separation. It was so easy to transfer a housemaid – only a signature from the Manager would make me redundant. Would Paul actually keep his promise to follow me, if this were to happen? And could I allow it, when he was enjoying his work at the factory, and must be certain of constant employment to provide the generous allowance he sent with such scrupulous regularity to Ireland every week? My relationship as the 'other woman' had no foundations. It was built on sand, and the tide of circumstance could wash over it, and destroy it, at any time. The truth must be faced, and pride condemned and deplored my precarious hold on this man. It was humiliating. At a time when I should normally have been wearing an engagement ring, and taking my man home to be approved by the family, I was obliged to hide the fact of Paul's very existence, to write letters every week in which no mention was made of this, the most important event in my whole life. It should have been a simple matter to allow the transfer to go through, to pack my case and move on, for I had spent the past ten years moving restlessly from place to place in search of something, or someone. But now, because I had found what I had been searching for, I wanted to stay in this one place, where he could be seen and touched, and loved every day.

The dread interview loomed as large and menacing as a thundercloud. What should I say? What excuses could I make for breaking the rules? How explain this sudden sweet awakening to love to a committee of men and women concerned only with morals?

'You worry too much, sweetheart. It's always a mistake to rehearse what you have to say. Let it come spontaneously. Be natural, be yourself,' Paul advised.

I left him sitting in the main hall, awaiting his turn to be interviewed, ready to enjoy every moment, for he loved an audience and the sound of his own voice! His conceit was as much a legacy of childhood – with an adoring mother and six sisters – as was my own honesty.

He kissed me, gave me a gentle push towards the closed door, and whispered, 'Good luck, my darling. I shall be waiting.'

I went in, and found myself face to face with a row of six

people, three men and three women. Four were familiar, two had come especially from London, for we were not the only offenders to be reprimanded and warned that rules were made to be kept, not disregarded.

'Sit down, Miss Shears,' said one of the strangers, kindly, indicating a chair.

What did I say? I have no recollection, for I said nothing of what I had so carefully rehearsed. Yet it seemed to satisfy them.

'Be natural, be yourself.' Perhaps Paul's advice was sensible, I shall never know whether he or I turned the scales in our favour, but we hadn't long to wait for the verdict. That same evening, a note was delivered to my room on Block Eight, and our two heads bent eagerly over the typed page. The items were listed.

'1. Paul Taylor is to be allowed to visit Sarah Shears in her room but must leave before 10 o'clock.
2. The electric fire may be used for heating food or making coffee, but a charge of 5/- weekly will be made for electricity.
3. Sarah Shears *must* take all meals in the canteen, when on duty.
4. Paul Taylor is asked to refrain from insulting the Welfare Officer.' (He shouted with laughter at this rebuke.)

Finally, I was thanked for my conscientious work on the Block, and the kind 'mothering' of the boys!

After three months of uncertainty, we now enjoyed the undisputed right to be together after working hours.

'Paul and Sarah, they go together like bloody bacon and eggs!' said one of my 'boys', indelicately.

We seemed to be living in a separate little world in Somerset, so far removed from the war and our families that I found it required quite an effort of concentration even to write a letter or make a 'phone call to someone beyond the scope of the hostel.

In many ways we were fortunate for, during those four years we lived in that community, we had no worries over ration cards, lodgings, laundry or entertainment. Everything was provided at a small inclusive charge to the factory workers, and free to the staff who had a proportionately lower wage. Cigarettes and chocolate rations were issued to coupon holders at the kiosk in the Main Hall, letters delivered and collected, library books exchanged and gramophone music provided in the canteen for those not already deafened by the clatter of plates, tin trays and cutlery!

In this sheltered little world, two lovers settled down happily. We must surely have been two of the happiest people there at that time; content with each other, with our work, and an environment that provided pleasure for Paul's gregarious appetite, as well as quiet lanes for my own solitary walks.

Walking was a pastime Paul regarded with suspicion. 'Where are we going, sweetheart? How far? Shall I be back in time to have a drink with the boys?' were questions likely to spoil a pleasant country stroll on a Summer evening. Fresh air was not as necessary to his city-bred lungs as it was to me. I marvelled at his splendid health and vitality, for he seemed to have spent most of his adult life indoors, and would not walk anywhere if he could find a means of transport. The half-mile walk to the factory, enlivened by the Major's springing step, was only endured because Paul was determined not to lose face.

'You see, my sweet, you have made a mistake. You should have picked on the Major, not me,' Paul teased, as we watched the tall, distinctive figure of his room-mate striding away down the road after Sunday dinner, while most of the boys were back on their beds!

'But I doubt if he stops to look at anything on the way. It's exercise he's keen on, not nature, and it would worry me having to keep up with him, and measuring the miles to beat last Sunday's record. No, I'll stick to my stuffy old Yank!' I told him – 'and anyway, I was under the impression you picked on me, that first day?'

'Only because that bitch of a housekeeper ignored me. I can't stand to be ignored!'

'So I've noticed.'

'I'm a conceited sort of guy – I want to be noticed.'

'Yes.'

'You missed your cue, sweetie. You were supposed to contradict me at that point.'

'The truth must be faced, my love. You *are* a bighead, in both senses of the word! Your mother should have called you

Caesar Augustus. Wasn't Paul a little man?'

'Which Paul? Now you've got me guessing again.'

'Paul the Apostle.'

'I wouldn't know. When you start quoting the Bible to me I'm completely fogged, for I can't remember a thing – only that yarn about Noah building an ark, and taking a lot of animals aboard. That rather appealed to me as a kid. It was a quaint sort of operation, with lions and lambs all living together in perfect harmony, so we were led to believe.'

'You're sceptical?'

'Sweetie, it's too fantastic – but it's a good story.'

'It could have happened. Nothing is impossible to God. And the rainbow is real enough.'

'Where does the rainbow come into it? You've got such a memory for detail.'

'At the end, when they are all safely back on land. It was the visible sign of God's promise – "I will set my bow in the sky, for while the earth remaineth, seedtime and harvest, and cold and heat and Summer and Winter, and day and night shall not cease," ' I quoted.

He stared at me in surprise. 'You're wasted on this job, sweetheart. You should be teaching at Sunday School!'

'A fine example! A Sunday School teacher's conduct must be above reproach.'

'Yes, I reckon so,' he sighed. 'You could try taking a class for the "boys" on Sunday afternoon. All those Bible stories and hymns should keep them awake!'

I knew if we kept on talking Paul would not notice the distance. It was an old trick I had discovered in the days when he first climbed over the gate with me to explore the wood and the lanes that I already knew so intimately. He was like the child I had once been, back in the hop-gardens of Kent, plodding over the clods to the accompaniment of the Cockneys' music hall songs. When we stopped talking, I would distract Paul's attention with 'Onward, Christian Soldiers' or he would chant a part of the Mass in Latin, and translate for me. His deep, resonant voice had a pleasing intonation that matched the solemn passages, and I was surprised to discover he was trained to sing this way by the Jesuit Brothers, and had remembered every word – as I remembered the Chapel hymns.

There is pleasure in the discovery of all these unsuspected talents and tastes in the beloved, for the mind must be explored as well as the body. Perhaps I was the more in need of the stimulus of an educated companion, while Paul would have been satisfied with the sensuality of the senses. I am still not sure. Certainly I could have wished that he shared my passion for books and reading, for the dark evenings would separate us for at least two hours, since he was too restless to settle down with a book. Opera was his only relaxation. Operatic music was not often included in the wireless programmes, but he never missed a chance to hear it, hoping for his favourite aria from *Turandot*, 'Nessun Dorma'. Even so, it was a strange kind of relaxation, to me, a stranger to opera, for his emotions were so stimulated by the music and singing that the tears would sometimes pour down his cheeks.

'Darling, you're crying!' I exclaimed, in dismay, the first time it happened.

He shook his head, speechless, and held out his arms to me, to lie beside him and share this extraordinary feeling of participation in the tragedy – for opera, I soon discovered, was usually based on some tragic tale of unrequited love. With my head on his shoulder, he continued to weep for the poor, unfortunate victims of a cruel fate, while I remained dry-eyed and unaffected by the intensity of feeling in the man beside me. No, it was not for me, and the only one for whom I felt any sympathy was poor, misguided little Butterfly, abandoned by the rascally Pinkerton!

I had fallen very low in the housekeeper's early estimation by associating with a married man. The bluntness of her Scotch tongue could be very hurtful. She thought I had been a 'wee bit hasty' in forming such an attachment with a total stranger, and she was disappointed in me, for I had seemed a sensible soul, she told me.

'Have you no' considered the future, my girl?' she asked, in the rich brogue of the North.

'Yes.'

'Does it no' bother you?'

'Very much, but I love him, and where he goes, I go.'

She shook her head at such foolishness. 'And his wife and child? Where do they come into the picture? You seem an intelligent woman, Sarah, but how can you reconcile your selfishness with Paul Taylor's responsibilities?'

'I can't. I'm ashamed, and it saddens me, yet I can't give him up.'

'Have you tried?'

'Yes.'

'It's because you're thrown together every day. If you were parted, and the attraction was removed, you could start a new life and forget this infatuation.'

'It's not infatuation. I thought it was when we first met, but it goes much deeper. I could never forget him, or love another man as I love Paul. It happens only once in a lifetime, I'm sure of it.'

She sighed in exasperation. 'Well, I suppose you are old enough to know your own mind, but you happen to be a member of my staff, and I feel a certain responsibility for you. I know you managed, between you, to convince the Committee that you had a legitimate right to be together after working hours, but I was not of that opinion, and I have no' changed my mind. Paul Taylor has a duty and an obligation to his wife and child, and you are preventing him from carrying out that obligation with a clear conscience. It would be an easy matter to arrange a transfer. Will you no' consider it?'

'I'm sorry, Mrs Mac, but I want to stay here.'

'You're an obstinate woman. To tell you the truth, I did'na think you would stick the job for more than a week when I first set eyes on you,' she confessed.

I brightened at her change of tone, and hoped she had finished the lecture, but she hadn't.

'There's a film you ought to see when it's shown here. It's called *Back Street*. It might convince you, since I can't,' she said, shrewdly.

I was silent, waiting for her to continue.

'It's the story of a woman in love with a married man. He had a good position, a luxurious home, an attractive wife, and two lovely children. He wanted to keep them all, and was not prepared to deny himself the benefits he had acquired, or the woman who was his mistress. So she stayed in the background, and for years he visited her in her shabby lodgings in a back street of the town in which he was quite a notable figure. That attachment, which neither had the courage to end, affected five lives, for the children became aware of their father's infidelity, and the wife was made miserable by her husband's deception. As for the woman – what sort of life would you call it? Would you agree that a few stolen hours of her lover's company, once a week, could compensate for marriage, a home and children?' she demanded.

I shook my head. Tears pricked my eyes. She had made it all so plain to me, in a final attempt to persuade me to change my mind, to accept the transfer to another hostel – to leave my dear love. I did not tell her I had already seen the film in London, and the story haunted me. It was so true to life, and a warning to those who thought it possible to combine the roles of husband, father and lover without detection, without heartbreak.

We did not realize that this early period of our life together would be the only settled and secure period we should ever know. For me, security was not an absolute necessity, for I enjoyed a challenge and a change, but Paul had none of my avid curiosity to look around the next corner, and like the majority of men who are not born adventurers, he liked security in his public and private life. This period was an interlude in his busy life, that postponed decision, and four years was a long time for a man of Paul's calibre to drift without ambition, without plans, without a sense of direction or achievement. He was strangely reluctant to talk about his early years, and I could only form a hazy picture of his life before we met – the father in the Diplomatic Service who died when Paul was a baby – the comfortable house in Washington – the Jesuit College where Brother James had taught his young, adolescent pupils the meaning of the word 'prostitute' as well as Latin and Botany – the commercial training and appointment to a large firm of textile manufacturers – his travels abroad and his meeting with Jacqueline (a model from a Mayfair salon) that day at the Dorchester, and his instant intention to marry her – the transfer to the Manchester office, because his wife refused to live in the United States – and the appointment to Company Director at the age of thirty-five. The luxury flat in a residential suburb of Manchester suited Jacqueline very nicely, but she hadn't wanted a child, and the marriage was on the rocks even before the child was born. They were too much alike, both self-important, quick-tempered and gregarious. The child was the bond that held them together, the one precarious hold on a marriage that could survive only by separation. They still were alive only because Paul had insisted that mother and child left Manchester for Ireland in the Autumn of 1939, and he himself was dining with a client in a city restaurant when their block of flats was demolished. After losing their home, he lived in an hotel, still working for the American firm until the fall of France ruined their Continental markets, and closed the Manchester office.

Jacqueline had shared her parents' home in the country, a few miles from Londonderry for a time. The child was happy in her new surroundings, but Jacqueline became bored and restless, and Paul soon realized she could not be expected to stay indefinitely in such isolation, with only a small child and elderly people for company.

During the first Christmas of the war, he had been to Ireland to see them settled in a flat in town, over a small hairdressing establishment. The owner, a widow of retirement age, was glad to sell the business to a client who made up his mind so quickly, and promised to come in every day to teach Jacqueline and keep the customers satisfied until she was proficient. It seemed to settle the problem, for at four years of age, Rosalinde would be accepted at the Convent kindergarten.

Every Sunday afternoon, Paul made a telephone call to Ireland, and, for me, it was another kind of torment that he would never understand, for he came back to tell me what the child had said to him, proudly reciting all her little accomplishments. Perhaps I was to blame for encouraging it in the beginning, but I was anxious that nothing should disturb this loving father-daughter relationship. Because the child was so important in his life, I had to try to understand, to put myself in his place. If the position were reversed, and I were the married partner with a child, would I not want to talk about her?

I knew I had not succeeded in my good intention when, for the first time in my life, I was jealous – not of the wife, but the child.

* * * * *

It was considered more economical to send all the workers on holiday at one time. So the factory and the hostel would close down, but for a skeleton staff, for ten days in August, at

Christmas, and Easter, and we were warned in good time to make private arrangements.

I was frantically busy for a week before the August holiday of our first Summer together, and the clothes line at the back of the Block was hung with shirts every day, dripping pools of water on the concrete path, for I was a poor wringer. Some of my 'boys' sent parcels of washing home every week, some did their own and draped it untidily around the bathrooms, and some came pleading, with their weekly ration of chocolate, and I found them and the chocolate hard to refuse! All the shirts had to be ironed, for the luxury of 'drip-dry' had not yet reached us.

As naturally as the average wife washes her husband's clothes, so I washed Paul's. The Major did his own, and was still a little haughty with me, for he considered I was entirely to blame for enticing a married man into my virgin cell! He would doff his bowler hat when we passed in the road and he thanked me politely for clean linen, but I still felt like a chambermaid, and I am sure he regarded me as a servant. But I was sorry for the poor chap, since it must have been extremely embarrassing at times to share a bedroom with a man like Paul. He would adjourn to the bathroom to dress and undress, in a long robe, and would remove his false teeth under cover of the bedclothes! Poor Major! But there was no alternative accommodation at that time, and, surprisingly, when it was offered at a later date, and single rooms were available, neither wanted to move.

All over the British Isles my 'boys' would disperse for ten days, and Paul would see the Irish contingent at Stranraer, waiting to board the mail-boat taking them home.

'I shall be away for ten days,' I heard Paul telling the Major. But he didn't say, as all the rest were saying, 'I'm going home.'

'This is my home now, on Block Eight, and you are my wife,' he told me on our last evening together.

'Don't call me by that name. I shall never be your wife!' I sobbed, miserably, for I could not see beyond the morrow and the parting, and I was terrified that he would not return.

I watched the dear, familiar face framed in the carriage door, and stood alone on the far end of a station platform. It never became any easier to bear, for the promise that he would return to me was not infallible. Anything could happen to detain him in Ireland. If husband and wife both lost their tempers and made a scene in front of the child, she would know the truth about her parents, or if the child was ill, he would stay with her.

'She is my child, and it makes no difference to us,' he had insisted.

But if he had to choose between us, after only three months of my acquaintance, he would choose the child.

* * * * *

'Are you doing any writing these days?' asked Mother, conversationally, as she mixed a cake and kept an eye on the two little evacuees, Charlie and Mavis, playing in the garden. The cake was the same mixture she had been making all her married life, but now, in wartime, she was using up a packet of stale dates in place of currants and sultanas, and powdered egg. 'Making do' was no hardship to Mother; she had known it all her life, for her childhood was as frugal as ours, and her own mother just as resourceful.

She was not really interested in the writing, and considered it a shocking waste of time when I could have sat for the Civil Service examination and spared her a lot of anxiety in my youth, instead of walking out of a job in the post-office in Brighton to take up work in Holland! But she hadn't seen me since April, and now I was home for ten days, and she was determined to make the best of her errant daughter!

'There is no time for writing, I'm too busy,' I told her.

'What do you do in the evenings? You can't be working all the time?' she challenged me.

She had taken her eyes off the children and the cake mixture, and they searched my face. I could feel my cheeks burning, and I answered her evasively.

'Oh, there's plenty to do – long country walks, film shows, concerts. Never a dull moment.'

'Have you finished that jersey you started for Charlie?'

'Not yet, but I'll finish it this week. I've brought it with me.'

'That's right. It's been hanging about a long time,' she said approvingly, scraping the sticky mixture into a cake tin burned brown with years of baking in the old-fashioned kitchen range of our country cottage in Kent.

The two evacuee children kept me busy all day, on that first holiday without Paul, and it was only at night, in the privacy of the spare bedroom, that I could indulge in a few tears, and wonder if I should ever see him again. I missed him intolerably, and ticked off the days on the calendar, longing for an end to an enforced holiday I could only pretend to enjoy.

'Well, at least I know where you are and what you are doing, during the war, and that's more than can be said for peacetime,' Mother told me, with a wry smile. 'This idea of the Ministry of Labour to keep a register of all single women up to the age of forty-five, and direct them into useful employment is the best thing that could happen to someone as restless as you, my girl!' she added, with a touch of the old severity. 'Just like your father – never satisfied, always on the move, and what do you gain by it, I should like to know.'

There was so much I longed to tell her – 'Mother, I've found what I was searching for, and I don't wish to move on any more, unless he and I can go together. Mother, I love a man called Paul Taylor, but he's married and he has a child. Mother, I'm sorry, but it just happened' – but I looked at her and said nothing, for she was too good, too straight, too sensible to listen to such foolishness. As a child, I always wanted to please her, but seldom succeeded. Now, as an adult in my thirty-fifth year, I still wanted to please her, yet I was farther removed than ever from her conception of rightness and honour.

* * * * *

He stepped off the train on to the platform, and as he walked briskly towards me, swinging the big suitcase, I was choked with joy and relief. When he caught sight of me, the wide grin spread over his face, and he waved as excitedly as a young boy greeting his girlfriend. I waved back, my heart pounding, my cheeks burning, till he dropped the bag at my feet and snatched off the Panama hat he had worn for the holiday.

'Sweetheart!'

'Darling!'

He was back, and I was enfolded in his arms, as the crowd surged round us.

'Kiss me!' he commanded.

The we laughed, with all our tension and anxiety forgotten, when he took my hand to join the long queue for a taxi to take us back to the hostel. We looked at each other, and saw nothing and nobody but our two selves, reunited.

'You see, it wasn't so long, my sweet,' he said.

'It was an eternity. I missed you, Paul.'

'I missed you, too.'

'How are they?'

'Very well, thank you - and your Mother, is she well?'

'She's well and happy with the two little evacuees.'

'How come you look so tanned?'

'I've been on the beach with the children every day. You look pale, darling. Have you been indoors?'

He nodded, his dark eyes held mine in a long, absorbed gaze while we went on talking quietly in the queue, moving slowly along the kerb, with no sense of time, but acutely aware of each other.

'Do you still love me?' he asked.

'Very much - isn't it obvious?'

'I wondered if your Mother would persuade you to change your mind.'

'I didn't tell her, she wouldn't understand. Did you tell Jacqueline?'

'No, do you mind?'

'I don't mind anything now you are back.'

'I told you I would be back. You don't trust me?'

'I was afraid the child would keep you. Did she cry when you left?'

'Not this time. Her mother was taking her to buy her first pair of ballet shoes. She goes to dancing class on Saturday mornings. I think it helped to take her mind off the parting.'

'What did you do all day, if Jacqueline was working?'

'Anything she wanted - Rosalinde always decides for both of us - shopping, cinema, shows, meals in restaurants, playing cards and drinking coffee - she makes very good coffee. I taught her,' he told me proudly.

It all seemed rather sophisticated entertainment for a small girl of six and, compared to Mother's evacuees, her tastes were certainly adult.

'Does she never want to go to the seaside, with a bucket and spade?' I asked, curiously.

'I wouldn't know. I guess nobody has ever suggested it,' he admitted.

His fingers entwined in mine sent a tingling sensation through my whole body, for even his fingers held a small measure of his strong sensuality, and he was impatient to lie with me. This sense of touch, so extraordinarily sensitive, renewed after ten days' separation, brought us instantly together again – a man and a woman, desperately in love.

'I must get properly organized on the food front,' Paul told me, determinedly, that first day back at the hostel, when the food revolted him more than usual after the meals he had been enjoying twice a day at the best restaurant in Londonderry.

'And you must support me, sweetie!' he added, meaningly.

'Oh, no, I won't be dragged into it,' I protested. 'I'm Staff and you're Resident, remember? A great gulf divides us, it seems, for you can still get away with murder, while I am reprimanded for being five minutes late.'

'It won't exactly involve you. I mean, I wouldn't expect *you* to cook the chicken. I would be the cook.'

'Chicken? What chicken? Is this another of your black market deals?'

'Yes, in a way – a chicken in exchange for a round of drinks, and perhaps a small little piece of chocolate for Ted's wife, at "The Plough", if she provides a few vegetables,' he hinted.

'Not even a small little piece. I need all I can get to keep up my strength for the chores.'

'But we must eat properly. Food is very important.'

'To you, perhaps, my love, but I was brought up on stews and suet dumplings.'

He shuddered. 'Poor darling.'

'Not at all. It suited me fine. See how healthy I am!'

He kissed the tip of my nose. 'Seriously, I must get my hands on a chicken.'

'Where? How?' I frowned at his persistence, but knew he would have his way.

We were standing together at the window of my little room, looking out on the familiar scene – groups of workers strolled aimlessly out of the canteen, and some of my 'boys' were drifting towards Block Eight. They were 'browned off' being back to the same old dreary routine.

'About that chicken, sweetie,' Paul interrupted my train of thought. 'I think I could get one to-night at "The Plough" if I went early. A local farmer keeps them supplied in exchange for an occasional bottle of whisky or gin. I might even get us a rabbit, later.'

Obviously he could not be side-tracked, so I had to take an

interest or seem ungrateful. He liked to visit 'The Plough' about once a week, to talk to the customers, for it was a change from the hostel bar, and the few topics the 'boys' were concerned about.

'Now all you have to do is to borrow a kitchen knife and a big stewpan,' he cajoled. 'Leave the rest to me.'

'I certainly will, for it's going to take all my powers of persuasion to borrow a stewpan. What do I give Maggie for obliging us?'

'Half-a-crown?' he suggested. 'We only want to borrow it.'

'If you make it five shillings, she might let us keep it.'

'Sweetheart! Don't tell me you're getting involved in all this bribery, after all?' he teased me.

'I suppose so. I seem to get involved with most of your crazy schemes. How long will it take to get this chicken?'

'Just long enough to stand a round of drinks to Ted and the customers.'

'It's going to be an expensive chicken.'

'It's going to be an appetizing meal by the time I've finished with it. Look at this? Doesn't it make you sick?'

The plate on the tin tray he had collected from the canteen contained a slice of fat pork in thin gravy, with two boiled potatoes and a sodden lump of watery marrow.

'Yes, it does,' I agreed. 'I swapped mine, at mid-day, for a second helping of prunes and custard. I can't digest pork.'

'But there's no vitamins in prunes and custard. No wonder you're such a shrimp,' he said, with a worried frown. 'How come you can't eat pork?'

'My darling, don't fuss. There are a whole lot of things I can't digest, but pork and pineapple would kill me. I repeat, I'm perfectly healthy.'

'You didn't tell me.'

'You didn't ask.'

We often arrived at this deadlock, I noticed, for we had so much still to discover about each other.

He left me at seven o'clock that evening, and by ten o'clock he had not returned. So I wrote a little note to slip under his pillow. He knew where to look, for we had arranged to do this if he was not back by the hour we had been permitted by the Management. The note was brief and rather curt, for I was disappointed not to see him again.

'Darling – if it takes three hours to get a chicken, how long will it take to get a rabbit? Good-night, Sarah.'

I found the chicken the following morning. It had been pushed through the open window, wrapped in a single sheet of newspaper. The blood had oozed through and I shuddered at the thought of the stew Paul would expect me to eat. A few onions and carrots, with a bunch of herbs, were also arranged on the window-sill, together with a note, much more loving than mine.

'My darling sweetheart – I do apologize for taking so long, and for not being back to say good-night. How come you can sleep when I've not kissed you? The chicken cost me a pound in a round of drinks, but it's worth it to get a good meal. Don't forget the pan and the knife. Sleep well, sweetie. All my love, Paul.'

The savoury smell of onions and herbs – the publican's wife had kindly raided her store-cupboard – attracted a lot of attention that same evening, and Bill, Joe and Taffy, my three favourite 'boys', collected outside the window, sniffing like 'Bisto kids'. Poor Taffy, whose wife had recently eloped with a Canadian sergeant, had come back from the holiday more gloomy than ever, after settling his three children with their grandmother.

'You're taking too many liberties, man, and Sarah's to blame for encouraging you. Is it chicken you're cooking, or permission only to warm up your dinner? he asked, in his singing voice.

'Oh, go to hell! – or come inside and stop moaning,' Paul snapped irritably.

Presiding over the stewpan, draped in an old towel, he was concentrating fiercely on a tasty meal, and didn't care for so many interruptions.

They wasted no time in argument, or the niceties of taking our food. Bill dashed to the canteen, snatched three plates and cutlery from the trolley, raced back, handed them to Joe to wash under the hot tap in the bathroom, who in turn handed them to Taffy to dry on the tea-cloth I was holding ready in the doorway. It was like a relay race, and they were very nimble, but even so, Paul was fretting and fuming that the food would be ruined.

'Buck up, you guys!' he yelled impatiently, and they clattered in like three boy scouts confronting the Scoutmaster, holding out their plates with sheepish grins.

'Is there a place to sit down, man, or shall we take it back to our bedroom now?' Taffy sang appealingly.

'Sit on the bed, for God's sake!' rapped Paul, ungraciously.

But by this time they all knew him so well, they took no offence from his barking. Not another word was spoken, however, until all their plates were cleared, and somebody belched comfortably from the other side of the partition. When I choked with glee over my portion of chicken, Bill stuck his head round the corner to say, appreciatively, 'You're a bloody marvel, Guv!' and Joe asked for a slice of bread to wipe his plate.

'It was terribly nice, and it's a champion you are with the cooking, sure to goodness,' said Taffy.

Paul was grinning amiably as he stood up to untie the string that held the towel round his waist, or where his waist should have been, for he was getting quite a pouchy stomach.

'Would you like some trifle, boys?' I offered, since the dish was already on the table.

'I don't mind if I do,' mumbled Joe.

'Okay,' Bill agreed, but Taffy, with his appetite satisfied, thanked me prettily, but thought it would spoil the taste of the chicken.

Several cracked saucers had recently come into my possession, so I collected the dinner plates and served up the trifle. Paul shuddered and shook his head at the odd concoction I called a trifle. It consisted of stale cake, pulp jam, thin custard and blobs of ersatz cream!

'But it couldn't have been too bad if Bill and Joe had two helpings,' I told him, after they had left. 'That proves nothing, sweetie. Those guys have no discrimination. They eat to keep alive, I reckon, and for no other reason.'

'Anyway, darling, the chicken was really splendid. They did so enjoy it.' I hugged him appreciatively, but he was looking at the bare bones, and wondering if hospitality had been extended too far.

'I had reckoned on chicken sandwiches for to-morrow night's supper, and some good soup for Tuesday,' he sighed, then looked at me with obvious intention. 'Let's go to bed, my sweet, you can wash up later,' and he locked the door on any further invasion.

As he pulled the blackout curtains, I caught a glimpse of the old, disarming grin.

'You owe me a cuddle, anyway, for inviting in those three guys.'

'But I thought you invited them?'

'Kiss me!' he commanded – 'and don't argue!'

* * * * *

And so the Summers of those four contented years faded into Autumns and the Autumns into Springs. The pattern of our days was so congenial, our work so satisfying, our love so increasingly fostered by our urgent need of each other, it seemed we were married and had lived together as man and wife for years. It was only the short holiday periods when Paul went to Ireland that brought uncertainty and sadness for me, in spite of Paul's reassurances that he would come back.

* * * * *

When Paul's mother died suddenly, at the age of eighty, and he read the sad news in a letter from his sister Louise, it was my turn to comfort.

'Why didn't I visit her again while I had the chance? It's seven years since I saw her last, and she has never seen her grandchild. How come I could neglect her all these years – my own mother?' he asked me, with sorrowful eyes and heart.

'Tell me about her, and your sisters. Tell me what it was like to be the only boy in a family of six girls,' I coaxed, and held his head to my breast, filled with compassion for a man who had left it too late.

'Mother was a dainty, fastidious little person. She wore rather fussy clothes and loved jewellery. My father adored her, apparently, and she liked a lot of attention,' Paul told me. 'My second sister, Bertha, is like her. She married a guy twenty years her senior, and they had no children. She's a widow now, with a lovely home in Florida and plenty of money. Annabel was considered the brainy one. She went to college and married a history professor. They have two sons and four grandsons, and live in Kansas City. Then comes Kitty. She was the naughty one, and always in some sort of scrape, I remember. She married the boy next door – a strange sort of guy, but a clever, scientific brain. They have always lived abroad, mostly in the Far East, and have a large family. I've lost count – seven or eight, I believe. Jessica and Margaret were twins, but not a scrap alike. Jess was my favourite. She was a terrible flirt, and used to bribe me to tell the old boyfriend she had a headache and couldn't come out, when she was already enjoying herself with the new one. All these five sisters bribed me with pocket-money when I was a kid. I guess Louisa, the eldest, who looked after Mother, never had time for boyfriends, but all the rest were courting, and I made a charge for delivering messages and playing the watch-dog. Oh, I was pretty crafty, even in those days!' He smiled whimsically at the memory, and went on, 'You see, Mother was supposed to have a weak heart, and they were all scared to upset her, so they had to do everything in secret, and depended on me as the go-between. Bertha was the prettiest, and had the biggest choice of beaux, I remember. She broke a few hearts when she married the guy from Florida, but he was the only one with a good bank balance, and Bertha was no fool.'

Once started on the family saga, Paul went on talking for some time, for he seemed at last to want to tell me about his family. It was a natural reaction to the shock of his mother's death. In this home, so predominantly feminine, I could imagine the young boy growing up bold and precocious, with all the flattery and attention, and very aware of himself as the only male. The discipline of school and the Jesuit Brothers must have seemed harsh to him, but it probably balanced the spoiling and formed his strong character. They were not a closely-knit family in adult life, and by the time Paul left college, five sisters were already married and scattered. Only Louisa, who never married, still wrote regularly through the years, giving him news of the rest of the family. Paul quickly scanned her letters, I noticed, smiled or scowled, according to the information they contained, then forgot them. But when the first half-dozen lines arrived from his own small daughter, there were proud tears in his eyes, and he carried the letter round in his wallet, with a snapshot of her in her new school uniform, for all the years we lived together.

His Easter visit to Ireland one year had coincided with the special occasion of the child's First Communion. He came back, silent and saddened by this event in the life of a young Catholic, in which the communicant receives gifts and homage after the sacred Mass. He had spent so much emotion he was quite exhausted, and his nerves had been strained to the limit in the effort to keep up the pretence of a normal relationship with Jacqueline. Together with the rest of the proud parents they were in the public eye all day, for the occasion has a significance far in excess of our Sacrament of Confirmation – though I remember my own nerve-wracked experience receiving the Bishop's blessing at the age of thirteen. These children were much younger, the average age being eight. All the little girls, dressed as brides, would suggest a sweet innocence and purity even to an outsider like myself, but to a parent, it must be pregnant with poignancy. To kneel in church, side by side with the child's mother when all love is dead between you would be heart-rending to both parents. For the sake of the child, the pitiful pretence of harmony is enacted with dignity and restraint.

'She passed by, in a procession of little girls, but I saw only this one child – my child,' he told me. 'She was close enough to touch, but I dare not touch her. She was not even thinking of me, or her mother, and her eyes were big with wonder. She was very pale, but her face had a kind of rapture. I was weeping, and her mother was weeping. Few of the parents were dry-eyed, I guess, as their children walked past, in a slow, solemn procession. Sweetheart, what have I done to her?' he asked, contritely – just as he had asked one May evening when he took me in the wood, 'Sweetheart, what have I done to you?'

How does a woman answer such crucial questions?

* * * * *

When the dark Autumn evenings brought a change in our routine again and electric fires were restored to all the rooms on the first day of October, I would go round the Block after tea, switch on the fires and pull the curtains, as I had continued to do through the four Winter periods we had already spent at the hostel. The boys were delighted to come home to a warm, glowing room, and soon spread the idea to other Blocks, where reluctant housemaids grumbled over the extra duty after they had signed off for the day.

'That Sarah Shears is always thinking up some blinking idea for spoiling that lot on her Block – the daft thing that she is!', I overheard in the linen room one morning as I waited for my quota of sheets, pillow cases and towels. But now, in the Autumn of 1945, all around us people were making serious plans. 'When the war is over' had a threatening reality now, and was not the vague possibility it once had been.

'What are you going to do, Guv? – here or Ireland?'

The boys also asked about me – questions that must soon be answered. They liked us both but were anxious about me 'spoiling my chances' with a married man. When the future was discussed in the bar or 'The Plough', or the Major brought it up on the evening walk from the factory, Paul would be very gloomy and silent, and would need several cups of coffee to restore his good humour.

I had long since discovered the best time to talk over a difficult problem or unpleasant topic was the half hour following our love-making, when he was particularly agreeable and relaxed!

'What *are* we going to do, my darling?' I began one evening, turning my head on the pillow to meet the glowing dark eyes.

His hard mouth was twitching with the indulgent smile he always had ready for me at such satisfying moments.

'Stay here – for ever!' he teased.

I sat up and begged, 'Be serious, *please*!', for the nagging anxiety had brought recurrent attacks of migraine.

'Lie down, sweetheart. I can't think straight when you are frowning at me.'

Was I frowning? I lay down obediently, waiting for him to speak.

'I want you both, you and the child,' he said at last, 'but it seems I can't have both – I have to choose to live with one or the other.'

My heart missed a beat, and an awful fear made me cry out in panic.

'Don't go! Don't leave me!'

His teasing sigh was more painful to me than any loud protest, but his arm tightened about my shaking shoulders.

'Don't cry, my sweet. I can't bear you to cry. There must be an answer to the problem, but I guess I haven't found it, *yet*.' He paused, and again I waited, whimpering with misery. 'Only two things are clear to me at the moment. I need you, and I must keep my child. I love you both, very much,' he added – and dried my wet face.

Paul was amused, at first, by my early Christmas preparations, for I always started knitting socks and gloves, as presents for the family and friends, in September. Wool was scarce, and only a limited amount could be bought when clothing coupons were needed to replace worn out garments. But when his fond caresses were rejected, while I struggled with the heel of a sock or a tricky thumb on a glove, he protested very strongly.

Paul, I think, in his impetuous way, would have liked to meet my family in those early days at the hostel, when he was still at the peak of his working life, robust in health, and obviously delighting in our relationship. But I was afraid, indeed I was certain that my brothers and sister still shared the same high principles as Mother, and would not hesitate to show their disapproval. I could imagine my elder brother, William – a bank official, on leave from the bank to serve in the Army in Italy – being very scathing indeed, and demanding of Paul some better arrangement for his sister in the shape of a marriage certificate! Henry, the younger, so bluntly forthright as to appear almost rude at times, would take it for granted that Paul would take the only decent way out, at the end of the war, and return to his wife and child in Ireland. As for Mary, she had always seemed so sensitive to family disharmony, and I thought to spare her the problem of deciding whether her sister should or should not live with a married man. Perhaps I was also anxious not to break the close bond between us. It was a combination of so many conflicting thoughts and intentions that prevented Paul from meeting them – a sense of disappointment that I could not introduce the man I loved as a future husband, pride in Paul that only I could admire and recognize.

By early December, the first Christmas cards arrived, so the window sill was cleared for the display. Paul sent money to Ireland for Jacqueline and Rosalinde to buy their own presents.

'But where's the spirit of Christmas, and the lovely surprises for a little girl? It's so meaningless,' I argued.

'They will expect it. I guess they prefer to choose their own presents, and it saves me the bother of shopping,' he told me.

But when he took two pounds from his wallet, one evening a week before Christmas, laid them on the table and said, easily, 'Buy yourself a present for Christmas, sweetheart' – I burst into tears, and pushed it away.

'What have I done now? Come on, you must tell me,' he insisted, looking very puzzled.

'I don't want money, Paul. There is no feeling in it, no sentiment – it conveys nothing, absolutely nothing!' I wailed. 'Couldn't you buy me a little present – anything – a surprise – not money!'

I tried to explain, but he still looked puzzled.

'Well, I reckon one of these days I shall understand you, my sweet, but I never knew a woman refuse money before,' he sighed.

The following day he came back with a bulky package.

'Open it – go on, open it up!' he demanded, impatiently.

'A brass jug! Paul, how lovely! Where did you find it?'

'In the village shop. The old dame told me it wasn't for sale. She used it to water her potted plants, but she changed her mind. I guess she was in need of the money. She sent the paper roses with her compliments for Christmas.'

The gift delighted me, but I had to keep the ugly, artificial roses till bluebell time for fear of hurting his feelings.

We were two of the last people to leave the hostel, for we both happened to have jobs that required us to complete a lot of work after our workers had left. For Paul, with the help of a secretary, it was records and details of several thousand redundancies. For me, with a block of rooms gradually vacated over a period of three months, it was just hard slogging, to leave the place clean, and beds stripped. We both found this period upsetting and depressing, for every week, as the redundancy notices expired, the atmosphere of excited anticipation soon changed to gloomy silence for the few who remained in the empty canteen, the bar and the Blocks.

My 'boys' left gradually, in small groups, and when I had cleaned their rooms and locked the doors, I felt very sad. But I kissed every one of them, including the Major, who was the first to leave! My three 'tough guys', Bill, Joe and Taffy, suddenly transformed into strangers in their utility suits and ties, with squeaking boots, were parting and going their separate ways. Bill was happy and confident. Joe wiped a sleeve across his wet eyes. Taffy sighed, and I listened to his sing-song voice for the last time.

'Well, it's lucky you are to have each other now, and I hope you will be terribly happy, sure to goodness, bach.'

At last the decision had been made.

We stood together, hand-in-hand, in the doorway of Block Number Eight, and waved them off in the hostel bus, then we went indoors.

'I feel like I had a pistol pressed to my head, and I'm scared to death,' Paul admitted.

'I am coming with you! My name is Ruth – where thou goest I will go!' I told him.

'Who is this Ruth? You talk in riddles,' he complained. Then he pulled me roughly into his arms. 'Now listen to me, sweetheart. Find us a home, any place, so long as we can be together. Okay?'

'Okay, darling,' I whispered.

2

The Cottage

I found the cottage, after much anxious searching, only a month before we were due to leave the hostel. Paul had taken no part in the search and seemed so uninterested I began to wonder whether he was not already regretting the decision to stay with me. What had he told them in Ireland? How did a father explain to a girl as young as Rosalinde that he was not coming back to live at home, but only for holidays? Had there been a dreadful scene with Jacqueline – or was she relieved? Paul refused to talk about it. We both were tense and nervous during this period, and the harmony was much disturbed by our separate problems. A frown, a cross word, and the tears were brimming. Finally, he lost patience with me, and who could blame him?

'How come you keep crying when I have told you I am not leaving?' he demanded irritably.

The decision that had cost him so much heart-searching had only increased my doubt, and I was still torn apart, not content and satisfied to accept his decision as a happy solution for both of us. There was still time to call up courage and pride – still time to release him from a promise he should never have made – still time to pack my case and leave him to make the journey back to Ireland, alone. But I liked him too much to let him go. In the past few years, he had become such a vital part of my life, I could not conceive a new chapter without him. He was my first thought on waking, my last thought before I slept – my reason for living, my joy and sorrow, pleasure and pain. The decision was made, and he had chosen to stay with me, but would he have chosen differently had I the courage to insist that we must part? Those few short months, when the lives of four people were so closely involved, and a little girl was asking her mother a lot of questions, changed the pattern of our lives so completely it no longer seemed possible to revoke the decision when that troubled period was past. It had a finality, but also a sense of sadness I could not dispel while we still lived at the hostel – and neither could Paul. We were back in the uncertain state of mind of our early attachment, four years ago, with the difference that Paul had since learned to say, 'Sweetheart, I love you, I need you,' as well as, 'I want you, Sarah, and you know it.' The difference was full of meaning to a woman who is always looking for signs and proof that she is loved. The proof, Paul declared, testily, was so obvious for the past four years, he couldn't make it any plainer had the town crier made a daily announcement!

But the seriousness of the step we were taking drained us both of gaiety and humour. The disarming grin was missing from that frank face, the eyes anxious with hidden thoughts, the mouth grim. My own feelings were so mixed and confused, my nerves so ragged, I had often to retire to bed with a migraine.

'Not again!' Paul groaned.

The house agent at Bath had warned me that it was too soon after the end of the war to expect to find a cottage in that part of Somerset, for so many of his clients had decided to stay in the country. Furnished lodgings were available in town, now that most of the aircraft workers had left, and he advised me to take rooms. But I could not imagine Paul in lodgings, and my own uncomfortable accommodation in a London apartment house before the war was an experience to be avoided if possible.

'I want a cottage,' I persisted stubbornly. 'I will 'phone you every day, and I shall be free to view at any time convenient to the owner,' I told the agent importantly, for now I could come and go as I pleased, providing my Block was clean and ready to hand over on the specified date.

When, at last, I set out by bus on a seven-mile journey north of Bath, clutching a large, heavy key, I began to feel the old urge to explore, the lost sense of adventure stealing over me. It was Spring again. The trees and hedges were budding, and I caught a glimpse of primroses on a sheltered bank, and celandines in a ditch. Through the open window I could smell freshly-ploughed earth, and new-mown grass in a cottage garden. Depression lifted and I looked about me with interest.

Here, in the open country, beyond the walls of the near empty hostel, life went on. If that chapter had closed, then I must begin to walk hopefully towards the new chapter, not dragging my steps unwillingly. It was my nature to walk hopefully, to look with interest and curiosity round the next corner – but I had always walked alone in the past, accepting and enduring all the disappointments and discomforts that came my way as part of the penalty of waywardness. How much could Paul endure, and would he find the adjustment to a new way of life too difficult? Could I alone compensate for the company of all the men at the hostel? Could I really expect him to be happy in a cottage? It would be another challenge, of a kind I had not intended, and would reject, even at this late hour, for anyone other than Paul.

Such were my thoughts as I stepped off the bus and walked briskly down the hill. The address the agent had given me was nearly a mile from the village and the bus stop, and the cottage was situated in a narrow lane, and had once been a farm cottage. The present owner paid the agent to collect the rent, and his name was not disclosed. It had been standing empty for some time, apparently owing to a cancellation. The lease would run for three years, with the option to renew, and the rental of £8 monthly had to be paid six months in advance – nearly £50. It seemed a lot of money. Could we afford it? How much money had Paul in reserve? Would he allow me to draw on my few savings to pay this initial sum, I wondered. More questions to be answered soon, perhaps to-day, for I had a strong feeling that my journey would not be disappointing, as I hurried down the lane still clutching the key.

It was exactly what I was looking for – a dream cottage for two lovers, and one a writer! Built of solid stone, mellowed with the years, it seemed to have taken root, like a tree, and was part of the quiet landscape, and the interminable tide of the seasons. The small windows were dirty, the garden a wilderness, the tiny front porch hung lop-sided on its broken frame. I stood on the threshold, trembling with excitement, but it took the weight of my two hands to turn the key in the lock, and the heavy, oak-panelled door swung slowly open on its creaking hinges. The smells that met my sensitive nostrils were easily recognizable – mustiness, mildew and mice!

The door opened directly into a small living-room, crowded with shabby furniture; the stove was huge, with two ovens, red with rust, and a greasy frying-pan, trampled by mice, stood on a pile of dead ashes. The last tenants had obviously been in a hurry to get away. Coconut matting was threadbare, and the springs of the sofa had burst through the cover. Oak beams supported the low ceiling. Would Paul crack his head? There were so many doors, I was curious to investigate. Where did they lead, and what should I find?

One led to a brick-floored scullery, listed as a kitchen on the agent's prospectus! Another led into the wilderness, described as 'half an acre of pleasant garden'. A third door opened into a cupboard, cluttered with old newspapers, chewed by the mice. The fourth door led to steep, twisting stairs, and two small bedrooms, sparsely furnished, and covered with cheap linoleum. Under the windows the wallpaper was peeling in damp patches. But I gaped and goggled at the vast double bed – the only piece of furniture in which Paul was likely to be interested! I tried to imagine the poor farm labourer's wife giving birth to six or seven children in this bed. Where on earth did they eat and sleep, and how many survived, I wondered.

The wide, uninterrupted view from the windows was untouched by the war, and everywhere I saw trees – in the lane, the garden, and the copse over on the hillside. Trees, books and flowers. I had to have them, and here I could have all three. For me it would be Paradise, but what of Paul? It was a risk I had to take, for the joy of having a 'place of our own'. With only a month to convert a dirty, neglected, four-roomed cottage into a home, I had to work quickly, for I still had to finish my work at the hostel.

Paul glanced up as I opened the door, and asked, 'You've found it?'

'Yes, it's perfect – well, I think so. Darling, it's a dream cottage, with a tangled garden and fruit trees, and a glorious view!'

'How much?' he asked, pointedly, cutting short my nicely rehearsed story.

'£8 a calendar month – six months' rent in advance, but a three-year lease.'

'Not bad,' he yawned.

'Darling, there's an enormous double bed with brass knobs!'

A slow grin spread over his pale face, and he pulled me on to his knees.

'I reckon we will take it, then, eh, my sweet? Kiss me! – then I'll write out the cheque,' he said.

Twice a week, during the following month, I made the journey to the cottage. The agent had his cheque, and I had the key – hidden in the woodshed. A home of our own, for three years!

A little of my excitement had penetrated Paul's lack of interest, and he asked a question from time to time, but was still much occupied in the office, and also with appointments for himself, since he was anxious to start on a new job as soon as we were settled at the cottage.

'What do we use for transport – buses or trains?' had been an obvious question.

'Buses.'

'Okay.'

'It's a bit of a walk to the nearest bus stop.'

'How far?' he demanded, suspiciously.

'Nearly a mile.'

'I'm not walking a mile to catch a bus. I shall take a cab.'

'Of course, darling.' I kissed him, and asked anxiously, 'Has the fifty pounds left you short of cash? I mean, you hadn't expected to pay out so much for rent this month, had you? Shall we manage till I find a job?'

'Job? What job? If you dare to mention working for a living I shall tan your backside!'

'I beg your pardon.'

'I should think so.'

Now that I knew how he would react to this suggestion, any future approach would have to be much more diplomatic – but perhaps I could settle down to writing?

'Won't it be cosy to have a real fire again. We must order logs and coal before the Autumn, but the last tenants have left us enough fuel to make a fire on chilly evenings,' I told him.

'Can't we have an electric fire to save all that work?'

'Later, perhaps,' I agreed, evasively – and quickly changed the subject!

Then, late one evening, he returned from his first interview at a civil aircraft factory, after taking a day off from the office.

I could see he was upset, and had no need to ask if he was successful. Sipping the strong, black coffee I had waiting, he suddenly exploded, angrily.

'Turned me down flat, sweetheart! Too old for the job!' He laughed derisively. ' "Too old? – but I'm barely fifty, man!" I yelled at that fool guy, and that didn't help any. "Doesn't experience count for anything? Do you want a young kid taking over your personnel department?" I demanded. But he was calm and cool as our friend the Major. "We are appointing younger men as heads of departments, Mr Taylor. Had you mentioned your age in your recent application I would not have asked you to call. It is the policy of my directors to engage ex-officers for their managerial posts, without any experience in industry or commerce. By that means we can train them to our own methods. I'm sorry, but quite frankly we just haven't anything to offer you." '

As Paul repeated this explanation to me, I was angry too.

'What utter nonsense! With all your previous experience, even before you came to Somerset, surely you would be an asset to any firm? It doesn't make sense. But don't worry, darling, for that's the opinion of only one firm, and it won't be general!'

He soon calmed down, but I knew he had been badly shaken by this first encounter with the problem, at a time when he was virtually in the prime of life.

'In future, my sweet, I am forty-five!' he told me, doggedly.

'Come to bed, darling. Forget it, for tonight. Tomorrow is another day,' I suggested.

It was a suggestion that a disappointed man would be glad to adopt so many times in the years ahead.

Sitting in the taxi that was taking us to our new home, we both felt so lost and abandoned we had nothing to say, and could only sit silently clasping hands, looking out at the landscape that was fresh to Paul, but already familiar to me. His face was so pale he looked quite ill, and his hand was cold and unresponsive. All my early doubts returned now I saw him sitting so dejectedly beside me. What was he expecting to find at the end of the journey? In this search for a home he had trusted me so implicitly. I dropped my head on his shoulder, and cried quietly.

'I feel like I was leaving home,' he said.

'I feel awful!' I sniffed, miserably.

When the driver had dumped our luggage in the front porch – I had fixed it rather clumsily with several large nails, and draped the clematis over the defects – Paul took the key and opened the door. The smells that greeted us now were clean and fresh – furniture polish, newly-washed curtains, and the flowers I had picked and arranged two days ago on my last visit. It was cosy and homely to my country-bred eyes, and I was pleased with my efforts. So much dust and dirt had accumulated under the matting I had to scrape the floor with an old knife before I could scrub, and everything, including the stove, shone with the vigorous polishing Mother had taught me in my younger days. 'Use plenty of elbow grease, child,' she would say.

But Paul had not noticed the clean smells, or the flowers. He had dropped his bags on the floor, and now he lit a cigarette and said, bluntly, 'I want to wash. Where's the bathroom?'

'We haven't one.' I was surprised to hear my voice so calm, and I had already recovered from my last attack of weeping. There would be no more tears from me for a long, long time!

'No bathroom?' he shouted. 'Then where do we wash?'

'In the bedroom. We have a china jug and basin, on a wash-stand,' I explained reasonably.

'And what kind of crazy system do we use for hot water and baths?'

'We have a copper for boiling water, and a zinc bath. We shall bath here in front of the fire, *once a week*.' Then, with a final fling of bravado, I added, wickedly, 'And the lavatory is down the bottom of the garden!'

I thought he was going to murder me there and then, and would probably dig a trench in the garden to bury my body, before setting out for Ireland. His eyes were blazing now, and all the apathy and depression was forgotten in this surge of angry resentment.

'My God! What a dump! – and I've paid the rent for six months!' he groaned – pacing up and down like a caged lion. He *was* a lion, and I had trapped him. 'Why didn't you tell me the truth?' he demanded.

'Because if I had you wouldn't have taken it, and I don't want to live in lodgings. I want a place of our own.'

He snorted indignantly, and puffed a cloud of smoke at the

blackened oak beams. I thought it best to ignore him until he cooled down a little – if he did cool down. In this present mood, he was capable of anything, and I wouldn't have been surprised to see him pick up his bags and walk out on me. So I picked up the bucket in the kitchen and made for the front door.

'Where are you going?' he growled. 'I suppose we have no water supply either?'

'Not indoors, but there's a tap down the lane.'

I pushed past his solid, masterful figure, ran down the lane, and filled the bucket. It was odd that I felt so happy and carefree, with Paul ready to murder me.

The fire was laid ready, so I struck a match to light it, while he watched every movement suspiciously from the sofa, where he now sat, looking extremely uncomfortable on the broken springs. Bright flames shot up the chimney, and the wood crackled. The room felt damp and chilly, and I sat back on my heels, holding my hands to the cheerful blaze, and said, 'That's better, isn't it?'

Paul made no answer. He was smoking his second cigarette, his forehead creased in a frown. When I had filled the kettle and stood it over the fire, I began to unpack the basket. The new coffee pot was a present from our three 'tough guys'.

'Got to have your coffee, Guv, wherever you go, I reckon, and you can't take that bloody great water jug!' Bill decided.

Paul had been very touched with the present. As soon as the first redundancy notices were posted, my 'boys' made a collection of cash and coupons, and I was presented with an enormous box of chocolates. I had brought provisions for several days, but it was coffee Paul needed now, not food.

Suddenly he got up, pushed open the back door, and strode down the garden path, between the tangled currant bushes and a forest of golden rod. He was going to find the lavatory! I wondered what scathing comments he would make on the little white-washed hovel, where large spiders ran up the walls? It was, however, smelling strongly of Jeyes, and not unpleasant once you got used to the spiders. But he didn't come back, and when I peered through the open door, I saw him standing quietly at the bottom of the garden, watching something very intently.

The coffee was brewing, and the strong, familiar aroma filled the room, and drifted out into the garden, but still he did not come. Then I heard a shout.

'Hi, Sarah! Come on out. We've got ourselves a squirrel!'

I went out quickly, delighted at the sudden change of mood, and handed him a cup of coffee.

'They're pretty mean with the crockery in this establishment – three cups without handles, six odd saucers, and four cracked plates! We really should take a trip to Bath one day, to buy a few odds and ends. I haven't got a decent broom, and there is only one chipped bowl, and. . . '

He cut me short. 'Sweetheart, I do apologize. I'm an ugly brute. Am I forgiven?'

I took his outstretched hand, and wound his arm about my neck.

'It was my fault, darling. But I honestly didn't expect you to be quite so shocked. I was so thrilled to get the cottage, these small inconveniences seemed unimportant.'

Then he yelled with laughter.

'Small inconveniences?' he echoed. 'If that's not a prize understatement, my sweet!'

And we stood there together, watching the red squirrel scurrying back up the tree. A pigeon cooed, and daffodils were blooming in the long grass.

'It's Spring again. It will soon be May – our month, and our Anniversary Day – remember?' I reminded Paul.

He nodded, and turned his head to look at me. 'That's one date I shall never forget.' He kissed me gently, and we sat down on a little bench under the pear tree, and stayed there, relaxed and happy till the shadows lengthened in the garden, and Paul shivered, then we went indoors.

'What are you thinking about so deeply?' I asked him, as I shovelled coal on the fire.

'That bed!' he confessed.

'But you've had no supper.'

'We can eat later. There's nobody to remind us when we must eat, or sleep, or make love!'

And he swung me up in his arms and carried me upstairs.

To-night, for the first time in four years, we were completely alone, and before his hard mouth closed on mine, he urged excitedly, 'Let's have a honeymoon, sweetheart! Let's not do anything else for a whole week but make love!'

I was smiling complacently now, in the big bed, with the brass knobs. The lavender satchets under the pillows and the freshness of sheets blown dry in the garden was sweet to my satisfied senses that night.

It was the kind of honeymoon that lives in the memory for a lifetime. We were free and happy, and so desperately in love. Time stood still for us for one short week. We slept, we ate, we made love, then slept and ate again! There was no plan or programme, no rules or regulations, no limit to our enjoyment of each other in this isolated place, where only the postman and milkman called, very early, without disturbing us.

I remember picking my first letter from Mother off the mat, and wondering if she was still annoyed with me for staying in Somerset.

'But what will you do in a country cottage if you can't make a living with your writing? Why not come back to Worthing, and look for a job, then you could write in your spare time. Keep writing as a hobby. Now Charlie and Mavis have gone back to London you could have their room,' she had written in reply to my rapturous epistle about a dream cottage I had found only a few miles from Bath.

I was sure that Paul had met with even stronger opposition from his young daughter, and possibly his wife, though I had a feeling she would not want to lose the independence she had enjoyed for several years.

I stood in the doorway, looking out on the tangled garden I would soon begin to tidy. The sun was warm on my bare feet, and a blackbird carolled in the old pear tree. There was no other sound, save the twitter of house-martins in the eaves. Everything had a lovely meaning and purpose, because Paul was asleep upstairs, and I had only to kiss his mouth to waken him, when the coffee was ready.

But this was my time to be alone for a while, when the clean sweet smells of morning rise from the earth, at the touch of the sun. Always my senses were most acute at this hour of the day, and feeling flowed upward from the earth, not downward from the sky. The sky was remote, and the moonlit nights sent shivers of wonder down my spine, but not warmth. Warmth, for me, came from earthy things, though I had, as yet, made no roots. This again was the element of contradiction, and the divided early loyalties to both my parents were still able to influence me, at different periods of my life, in different ways.

Now I was wholly my mother's daughter, born of country people. Restlessness had given way to contentment, and it was not entirely of Paul's making. The tenants who had left behind only dust and dirt and bad smells, had not cared enough to touch the garden, or mend the broken porch. They had used the place, but not loved it, for that was obvious even to Paul.

'They must have scratched their legs on these bushes when they went to the lavatory,' said he, chopping at the prickly branches with a blunt axe he found in the shed. I had since told him about the mess they had left, and my efforts to get it ready before moving day, for now it could be told with amusement. He was so contrite, so really determined to make amends for his foul temper that day. I found him in shirtsleeves one afternoon, digging a pit at the bottom of the garden. (We had no cess pool.) It was, however, his first and only attempt at manual labour. The chopping of wood, the filling of coal and water buckets, digging the garden, cutting grass and hedges, laying paths, and repairing fences kept me busy and strengthened my muscles!

Paul was the cook. I was the gardener-handyman. It was a natural assumption, and again, there was no compulsion. Instinctively he went to the kitchen, while I went to the garden; he stayed indoors, I went out. But for this first week in our new home, meals were most erratic. Paul would be cooking omelettes at three in the morning, or frying onions at tea-time! Day and night had no definition, and the week was a flowing, continuous period of time, in which we indulged ourselves and each other, abandoned our problems, and lived extravagantly on the large basket of food we had brought from the hostel. The Manager had taken a personal interest in what he called 'our daring decision to set up house together'. The housekeeper also had a change of heart, and gave me several patched sheets, towels and pillowcases, for we had no linen to start our housekeeping, apart from a couple of teacloths, a check tablecloth, and an old rug I had used on my travels before the war. With the dispersal of staff and residents, such unexpected gifts were possible, and we both were grateful to leave with their blessing, rather than the critical condemnation we had expected.

'One of the first jobs I must do, even on my honeymoon, is to make a bonfire and burn up all that rubbish I turned out of the shed, and the cupboards,' I told Paul, as he settled down to dicing vegetables for the next meal.

'Okay,' he grinned affably, '– but don't run away, I might want you!'

'You couldn't? – You wouldn't – not again?' I retreated hastily to the door with an armful of the dirty newspapers the last tenants had left behind.

'Isn't it time we took a bath, my sweet?' he suggested meaningfully.

'To-night,' I promised. 'When I've started the bonfire, I will fill the copper, but you must empty the bath when we have finished. Are you listening?'

'Yes, I'm listening. I can hardly wait for you to scrub my back! You never came near me at the hostel, I noticed, when I was taking a bath – how come?'

'The three "boys" might have started queueing for their turn!'

'Wonder what they are doing now? They were always your favourites.'

I nodded. 'Yes, and I had decided not to have favourites when I started on that job, but they seemed to need me more than the others, especially Taffy.'

'Is it a mistake you are making with Sarah so fond of you now, I am asking you, man?' sang Paul, in Taff's voice; and I went out laughing into the garden.

Laughter spilled out of us all that week, and we both recaptured the element of gaiety we had lost for a time. The bath was a riot, and we took our turn in front of the blazing fire, late at night.

'Where do I put the water when we are finished, if we have no drain?' Paul asked me.

'Tip it out on the garden, of course, where else? You've been so spoilt, darling, with all your daily baths, and now you are rationed to only one a week.'

'With all this work to take a bath, I reckon once a week is enough,' he sighed, filling up buckets from the copper.

'What a fuss you make over everything! We bathed this way every Saturday night till we went to Worthing. I was over twenty when we had our first bathroom,' I reminded him.

He had washed my hair in the bedroom basin because, he said, it stank of bonfires. I enjoyed having it washed, for it was a job I disliked doing for myself. The shampoo smelt of lemon, and brought back memories of Paul's arrival at the hostel.

'It was one of the first things I noticed about you, sweetheart. Your hair was naturally curly, not permanently waved, and smelt of lemon. A clean, sweet-smelling girl, I thought to myself. My! My! – not even a lipstick!' he mocked me, rubbing my hair dry with a warm towel.

There was some speculation in the village, apparently, over the new tenants at Willow Cottage, for the postman had reported delivering letters to a Mr Taylor and a Miss Shears.

'I can be the lodger, sweetheart, and you the landlady!' Paul had told me gaily, dismissing the problems so lightly I was astonished at a man's assessment of a woman's most urgent needs.

We had enjoyed the privilege of being together for four years at the hostel, openly, not secretly. It was an accepted fact that Paul and Sarah were lovers. Now it suddenly became necessary to establish a definite identity, for quite obviously I was not Paul's wife with a name like Sarah Shears! The first indication of the postman's natural curiosity arrived with a parcel from Worthing.

'You Miss Shears?' he asked, bluntly, when I opened the door.

'Yes.'

He looked me over with calculated interest and I knew I was blushing.

'That's all right,' he said. 'I just wanted to be sure it was being delivered to the right person. A Mr Taylor lives here too, I understand?'

'He does.'

'That's okay.'

'Thank you.'

I closed the door hurriedly, and stood there with my arms wrapped round the parcel, trembling with indignation. How dare he insinuate I was not married! It was more hurtful than a hard smack on the face, for I was not yet prepared to meet this new challenge the postman had flung at me.

'Living in sin,' his tone implied. Could anything be farther from the truth, if I searched my own heart? Yet it had to be faced, and my cheeks burned as I unwrapped the parcel – two sheets, two pillow-cases, two towels, and a white starched tablecloth – from Mother's own meagre supply of linen. She had at last accepted the fact that I was determined to keep the cottage as long as possible, but would visit her every third month. But I must feed myself properly, and make certain everything was nicely aired, she insisted. Living in sin? – All that day I was reminded that I must be ready to encounter other suspicious people, not only the postman. The battle we had fought at the hostel for the right to be together was won, and we were left alone. Would there be no end to the battles I must fight to keep my love in the future? Would I be branded for ever as a 'bad' woman for living with a married man?

'Paul, darling, we must talk about the problem,' I began – sitting on the edge of the bed, with the linen draped over the brass rail.

'What problem, my sweet?' said he, sipping hot coffee, with *The Times* and *Daily Telegraph* spread on the bed.

'What to call myself?'

'That's no problem. Mrs Taylor, of course.'

'With all my correspondence addressed to Miss Sarah Shears?'

'You're a writer, aren't you? That's your writing name. Actresses and writers always use their maiden name or a pseudonym. What does it matter? What's in a name? Don't look so worried, sweetheart.'

'It does matter to me – but I hadn't thought of that. You are so quick with your solutions, darling. I fumble and blush, and look guilty, when the answer is there!'

'It's simple,' he grinned – 'Mrs Taylor in private life, and Miss Shears in public.'

'Then shouldn't I be wearing a wedding ring?'

Now he yelled with laughter, and snatched me into his arms. 'I will buy you a ring. I will buy you anything you want, sweetie, even a marriage certificate, if it were possible, and if it would make you any happier. Now go away, Mrs Taylor! I must concentrate on these "ad" columns. With two wives to support, and two homes, I had better get cracking on a job – but it was a marvellous honeymoon, sweetheart!' he added wickedly, and pushed me away.

I went downstairs, wishing I had his ability to see things differently – to segregate the practical and the emotional issues, and to organize my life with more effectiveness. But perhaps it was a man's prerogative? For Paul, the decision was made, and the issue settled. We were living together, and the matter of a ring or a marriage certificate seemed trifling.

'My darling, you are my wife and I am your husband. What else can I say?' He always answered me so frankly, and I knew he was sincere, but it was not the answer a woman hopes for and expects. He seemed utterly and completely satisfied with the arrangement, while I secretly yearned for all the trappings of a formal wedding – the white dress and veil, flowers, bridesmaids, church bells and wedding cake. We had the honeymoon, but no wedding. There would be no photographs for the family album, no cherished tokens to keep for my children, for there would be no children. It was mocking the sanctity of marriage, and the earthly family of father, mother and child, fashioned on the Holy Family of Joseph, Mary and Jesus, for whom I had more reverence than Paul, though he was a Catholic, born of Catholic parents.

'I am worried about taking Communion, Paul,' I had told him, four years ago. He had shrugged, indifferently.

'It would be hypocrisy, wouldn't it?' I pressed.

'I don't see you as a hypocrite, sweetie.'

'No, because you are prejudiced in my favour, but if you were a priest, wouldn't you deny me the Sacrament?'

'I should if I knew, but you would have to tell me at confession.'

'And it would be regarded very seriously?'

'Yes, you would be forbidden to take the Sacrament.'

I sighed. 'That's what I wanted to know. I shall go to Church, but not stay for Communion.'

'Poor little sweetheart, I seem to be responsible for a good many changes in your life,' he said, but there was no regret or anxiety in his voice, only a rather smug satisfaction. He was still 'Master of his fate, and Captain of his soul' and the teachings of the devout Jesuit Brothers had been discarded, long since. Only the secular learning was retained – the Latin, the fluent French and German, geometry, mathematics, botany, and other subjects of which I had no knowledge at all.

* * * * *

The little pub, half-a-mile from the cottage, was called the 'Adam and Eve', and a 'phone box on the forecourt was Paul's only means of direct contact with the outside world until our own telephone was installed. It was, Paul insisted, a necessity not a luxury, but since his definition of necessity differed so widely from mine, I did not argue! A daily walk to the telephone, and a friendly chat and drink with George, the publican, and his wife, Mabel, was part of his new routine.

'Back to work today, sweetie!' he had announced, briskly, one morning, reaching out for the papers I had asked to be delivered every day. He was washed, shaved and dressed before I had time to clear the dead ashes from the grate. But I soon had a pot of coffee on the hob, and a bright fire burning, for the weather had changed and a grey sky darkened the room. The fire was cheerful, and Paul would need a bit of cossetting now, with so much on his mind.

Sheets of foolscap paper and large envelopes were spread over the table, while he copied out testimonials in his fine, flowing style, meticulously exact in data. His mind was cleared of honeymoon indulgences, and his earnest face, bent over the papers, was tense with concentration. He did not glance up as I went past, so I took my breakfast tray upstairs, and sat, looking out of the window at the leaden sky, thinking about the future, wondering how Paul could possibly manage to keep two wives and two homes on one salary – unless he allowed me to work. Independence was still sweet to me, but now, for the first time in my working life – and I had been working since I was fourteen – I was earning no money, and had no job. The several small markets I had managed to acquire for my stories in London, before the war, had dwindled away when these periodicals ceased publication because of paper rationing. It would mean a fresh start, and a new assessment of markets, for while I had been busy at the hostel, other writers had captured all the juvenile markets – the only market for which I had intended to write. Several unsuccessful attempts at a pre-war novel had ended in the waste paper basket, poems had been rejected, and song lyrics lost in the dustbins of 'Tin Pan Alley'! But if Paul was so strongly opposed to my working for a living in the outside world, I must work at home to earn a little pin money. Housework and gardening would not be enough to occupy all my time, especially if Paul had to be away from home during the week.

'Keep your writing as a hobby, for it's too precarious as a living.' Mother's sensible advice would be ignored again and again, for writing was as much a part of me as my limbs, and one cannot make a hobby of an obsession. Whether I succeeded or failed, I had to write again, soon. But it would matter a great deal to Paul if I failed to earn any money with my pen, for he regarded any work not rewarded by financial gain as a waste of time and energy. That an artist could create purely for his own enjoyment, on paper, canvas, or musical instrument, was something Paul would never understand. But because he loved me as a woman, he was prepared to accept the artist in me, conditionally, on his own terms. It must not interfere with my normal duties as a wife, or make me less ardent as a lover! It so happened that I could combine all three, but it still had to be proved, and that would take time.

Top priority, at the moment, was Paul – Paul's job and Paul's responsibilities in Ireland.

'Sweetheart! Go to the village and post these letters for me, will you, and buy some more stamps. You could ring the telephone manager while you are there, and tell him we are still waiting for our 'phone to be connected. Tell him it's urgent – *top priority!*'

'Yes, darling.'

One day, perhaps when Paul was back in an office, I would start on the stories, but not yet, not to-day!

For the following three months the tensions of unemployment and frustration made Paul irritable. Again I could see him as a lion, in a cage too small for his size and strength. He was straining at the leash, eager to reach the outside world, to use his mind and suppressed energy on some absorbing new work. The quietness of our surroundings was harmful, not helpful, in this present period of adjustment, and he would probably have been less conscious of tension in a tenement flat, or back at the crowded hostel. It was a time for action, not silent contemplation of the future, and he had already plunged into the tangled web of pretence by allowing his wife and daughter to assume that an important job was keeping him in Somerset, and by drawing money from the bank to pay their regular allowance.

I began to dread the postman's knock, and the letters I picked off the mat which invariably began 'Dear Sir, We thank you for your application and beg to inform you that you are not on the list of applicants selected for interview.'

When the written applications were unsuccessful, he began to telephone for appointments, and his diary was filling up with engagements now, while he travelled as far as Exeter, Salisbury and Reading, as well as covering the areas of Bath and Taunton. These appointments gave us both a welcome respite from the strain of waiting for news, for he would set off eagerly, by taxi, to catch a train from Bath, and hadn't to bother with tedious bus journeys, knowing he could charge up travelling expenses. Immaculate in a dark tailored suit and homburg hat, with a brief-case for documents, he looked so buoyantly confident, I knew he must make a favourable impression, and if he failed to get the job it would not be for lack of confidence or for slovenly appearance.

At the garden gate, his lips would brush mine in a glancing kiss, his face alert, his eyes alight with the excitement of another challenge.

'Keep your fingers crossed, sweetheart!'

'I'll say a little prayer for you, darling.'

We always exchanged the same sentiment in parting – crossed fingers and the prayer linked together in hopeful anticipation. *This* time he will be lucky. He *must* succeed to-day, I would think, as he strode briskly down the path to the waiting taxi, and turned to smile and wave.

I welcomed these interviewing days, for I could stay outdoors, have a picnic meal in the garden, and spend most of the day weeding and digging. It was hard work clearing the wilderness, but rewarding to lean on my new spade, to admire a small plot freed of the tangle of thistles and dandelions, and the strangling hold of bindweed. All through the lovely month of May the shrubs were sweet with white and purple lilac. Tulips followed the daffodils. Someone had loved the garden before the war, and planted a lot of bulbs.

In June, I found a bushy peony plant, its huge, floppy blooms hidden in the leafy foliage, and a fuchsia smothered in golden rod. Several small rose bushes stretched and reached for the light, as I cleared away the weeds. It was, for me, as exciting as Paul's interviews, this wonderful discovery of a garden that first Summer at the cottage. Hollyhocks grew tall against the old stone walls, and nasturtiums spread themselves over the rockery. Rambling roses trailed over fences, and the scent of lavender mingled with the scent of the roses was sweet to a country-bred woman.

The friendly red squirrel would watch my labours with bright beady eyes, and a robin followed me round, perching on the spade when I left it for a moment to use some other tool.

We had made a journey into Bath on the last day of the honeymoon, and Paul had bought crockery and cooking utensils, brooms, buckets, garden tools and deck chairs.

'What's this old lot of rubbish, then? You moving house or something?' grumbled the taxi-driver, who preferred passengers with only one suitcase. Paul also bought a wedding ring, some scented soap, and a large sponge for bath nights! It was the final fling of honeymoon madness, and our shouts of laughter echoed across the fields, as we unpacked the queer assortment of packages, and I rushed into the garden to experiment with the new tools. Then the seriousness of the situation became too pressing for Paul to linger any longer in a fool's paradise, and he closed the door abruptly on fun and frivolity. There were no half measures with Paul, and every day brought the same fierce concentration of thought and effort towards employment. It had to be an interesting, well-paid post, for his sake and ours – the two women and the child for whom he was responsible. But he was not a patient man, or a tolerant one, and his temper exploded in a burst of angry resentment over the formal, politely-worded letters that followed the interviews.

'Dear Sir, we beg to inform you the post is now filled. Yours faithfully.'

'Dear Sir, With regard to our recent interview, it has been decided to offer the vacancy to a younger man. Yours faithfully.'

'Dear Sir, We feel your talents would be wasted in the post we have to offer. Yours faithfully.'

'Yours faithfully!' he mocked, bitterly. 'These damn fool guys don't know the meaning of the word!' – and he ripped the letters apart and tossed them into the fire.

But he knew, and I knew, the main reason for all these

rejections was age. Even by calling himself forty-five, he was still too old, and his head was balding. It added to his distinctive appearance, but not to his chances of employment. And he was not British. Why did he not return to the States? He was questioned repeatedly about his nationality, his reasons for staying in England, his wartime activities, and his politics – all subjects that appeared to have no bearing on the appointments.

I watched him with growing anxiety, for now he was driving himself too hard, and the confidence had a brash bravado that hid the fear of failure. All his efforts in the past had been rewarded by success. He was puzzled and indignant at so much opposition to his plans. To keep up the pretence of occupation, he left for his normal ten days' holiday in August, with several more interviews arranged for September.

For the first time since we met, I hadn't to stand on a station platform watching the train slide away. I could kiss him goodbye at the garden gate, and the scent of honeysuckle was sweet on that Summer morning. Mother was expecting me in Worthing for a week, and I had to be prepared to play my own game of pretence, and be constantly on guard lest some chance remark would reveal the fact that I was not living alone. I hated this deception, and longed passionately to be honest and truthful again. Mother had never been a confidante in my adult life, but I still admired her wonderful qualities of courage and endurance.

I watched her from an upstairs window early one morning, hanging washing on the line. She liked to get some of her chores done before breakfast. All her movements were regular, her manner calm, her gestures completely natural. Choked with tears, I was remembering so many things as I watched her, unobserved, that Summer morning – remembering her courage when Father died in Baghdad – remembering her voice calling me back from the brink of Eternity after my third major operation at the age of fourteen.

'Sarah! Sarah!' – her hard, work-stained hand fastened on mine, her face, etched with lines of care, swimming into focus, and her dark eyes, imploring me to stay.

Nearly twenty five years ago, and I remembered that moment, as I leaned on the window-sill, watching her pegging the washing on the line.

And every mile of the journey back to Somerset I was

reminded of her, for the fields of golden corn were ready for harvest, and she was a farmer's daughter, with her roots in the soil of Surrey.

* * * * *

'We've had a proper showdown, sweetheart. For the child's sake, I had hoped to avoid it until she was a bit older, but it flared up so suddenly the first evening, it couldn't be avoided.'

Paul's face was strained and pale as he stepped off the train, but his greeting was as warm as ever. When we had settled in the taxi, and my hand was firmly grasped, he began to tell me about this disturbing holiday. Perhaps he was partly to blame, being so tense and anxious about the future and his manner may perhaps have been abrupt or absent-minded. But I think Jacqueline was probably ready to tackle him over his decision to stay in Somerset, since he had avoided it at Easter. If she had agreed, when the child was small, to keep her in ignorance of the estrangement, she may have been tired of the pretence, and who could blame her? I can only guess at the reason, but I could imagine the painful scene Paul described to me, and my sympathy was shared among them – father, mother and child – especially the child. A girl of nearly eleven years of age is usually an emotional creature, demanding answers to so many questions.

'The first thing I noticed when I saw them standing on the platform was Rosalinde holding her mother's arm, not her hand, and she didn't run to meet me as usual, but waited for me to join them. She still gave me a throttling hug, but the difference was there, sweetie – a kind of restraint in her manner, I reckon. My little girl is growing up too fast, I thought, and the change in her saddened me a little.'

I squeezed his hand, and he went on, 'We linked arms and walked away together, the child between us, then she turned to me and said, half jokingly, "Mummy is very annoyed with you, Daddy. You had better watch your step!" "I am not surprised, darling. Mummy has every reason to be annoyed," I told her, appeasingly, but now I was getting really worried, for her mother's fixed smile was more forced than usual, and I couldn't trust her not to make a scene. We had always tried to keep a tight rein on ourselves in front of the child, but I often got a ticking off when we were alone,' he confessed, with a wry smile.

'When we sat down to our first meal together, and she put a dish of salad on the table, I could see her hands were trembling, and her face was dead white, so I knew what to expect,' he sighed, looking straight ahead, avoiding my eyes.

' "Well, Paul, we are waiting to hear what excuse you have cooked up this time, and you needn't bother with the old excuse of better opportunities in Somerset than in Ireland, for I just don't believe it!" she told me, and I just didn't know how to answer her, with the child staring at us in amazement. "For once in your life, Paul, tell her the truth – or shall I tell her?" Jacqueline shouted at me. That shook me badly, my sweet.'

He paused, frowning, remembering every detail, and I waited, loving him more in his stumbling explanations than in his brash boasting.

'She didn't wait for me, she blurted it out, and that was cruel – cruel to the child.'

'What did she say?' I prompted gently.

'That I had been deceiving them all the time, and had no intention of coming home after the war. That I had no love for them, and had another home in Somerset – and I was a very selfish man.'

Now he turned to look at me at last, his eyes heavy and shadowed. I was dragging the story out of him now, but I had to know how it finished, for I was a part of it.

'Go on, what did you say to that?'

'Nothing. I got up and went out, else I might have hit her, I was so mad. Rosalinde was sobbing when I left the room, and she called after me. I stayed out, drinking, in the nearest bar. When I got back to the flat, I found them in bed together, sleeping in each other's arms, so I sat alone in the kitchen, drinking black coffee, as miserable as hell. Then I lay on the bed in the room they call "Daddy's room", and I suppose I dozed off, for when I opened my eyes it was daylight, and the child was sitting quietly on the end of my bed. She was very pale and subdued, and we just looked at each other, without speaking. Then I opened my arms and she slid into them, and cuddled down.'

He was not thinking of me now. I was just a hand to hold – a listener to a tale of a father's tumble from a pedestal his own child had created. The image was broken, but they would still adore each other.

Then she had asked him, pitifully, 'It's not true, is it? You do love me, don't you, Daddy?'

And he had assured her, 'Yes, darling. I love you very much.'

'"Why don't you love Mummy any more? I don't understand. She's the best mother in the whole world."'

'"Of course she is. One day you will understand that sometimes mothers and fathers stop loving each other, but still love their children." That's what I told her, sweetheart. What else could I say? She's still a little girl. But I reckon I made a hash of it, for she looked so puzzled.'

'You did your best,' I said, but it seemed to me a poor sort of explanation to a child of that age. 'How did the rest of the holiday go, after that bad start?' I asked him, and his answer surprised me, for it was an extravagant gesture while he still had no job and no regular income.

'I took her to London, and we stayed at Brown's Hotel for a week, just the two of us. I wish you could have seen her face when I suggested it. "But can you afford it, Daddy?" she asked me, and I told her it was a treat to make amends for her disappointment. I couldn't bear she should think so badly of me, and she loves surprises. When she was a small little girl, we sometimes took a ride on top of a bus, or went to the Zoo. We've had a trip on a speed boat at Blackpool, and eaten spaghetti in an Italian restaurant, just the two of us. Once I took her to Paris on a business trip, and she loved every second.'

Now his eyes were moist with nostalgic memories of the little girl who had taught him the meaning of tenderness – and a stab of jealousy reminded me that he never suggested to me that we stay at Brown's Hotel, or had a holiday together. I was the one who was left behind, to welcome him back with open arms. It was my turn to sigh, but I listened patiently because I loved him, and had to try to understand this other love for his daughter.

'Will Mummy mind?' had been the child's first reaction to the proposed trip to London. But there was no objection from Jacqueline, and it was quickly arranged. Two of the Convent sisters were already in London, attending a conference, so Rosalinde would travel back with them.

'And Jacqueline – how did you leave her?'

'Okay,' he said, carelessly.

I was curious about this woman he once had loved and

desired – the mother of the child. He was still thinking of the child.

'Rosalinde told me I ought to apologize, then her mother would forgive me, so I went right along and apologized. But I can't figure it out, my sweet. Was I apologizing for staying in Somerset, for being selfish, or things in general?'

'I wouldn't know. It's too complicated.' I smiled at the question. We were nearly home, and he hadn't even asked if I had enjoyed my holiday.

'She's a cute child, that daughter of mine,' he was saying. 'Her last words to me, before I handed her over to the Sisters, prove she was still thinking about the trouble. "I won't tell anybody, Daddy, not even my best friend – about us, I mean," she told me.'

'That was a nice thing to say.' My voice must have betrayed my own disappointment, for now he gave me his full attention at last.

'Well, my darling. You're looking very pretty in that new hat – how come you haven't kissed me?'

The bulbs were planted, and the smoke from the last bonfire drifted over the hedges, but still Paul was looking for a job. When the rains of late Autumn swept over the fields, I saw him standing at the window, looking out at the transformed garden, yet not seeing it, for there was desolation in his heart, and fear in his eyes – fear of failure. But I was still hopeful. Like Mr Micawber, I fully expected 'something to turn up', but Paul was sceptical of such persistent optimism. He wanted proof to substantiate my faith in miracles.

Now he was so tense and nervous I had persuaded him to walk to the 'Adam and Eve' twice a day, to spend an hour or two in the cheerful company of George and Mabel, and the customers. I would watch him hurrying back from the lavatory at the bottom of the garden, hunched under an overcoat in the rain – a figure of such abject misery, I was tormented with doubt over the suitability of the cottage.

'Oh for another week at Brown's Hotel!' he said, longingly, one soaking wet afternoon. And I put my arms around him, and coaxed, 'Come to bed, my love.'

It was November now, more than six months since we left the

hostel, and soon it would be Christmas again, and separation. It was still impossible to settle down to writing of any detailed length and concentration, but I managed to write a short story on Paul's interviewing days, for the gardening was finished till the Spring. Even this private activity had to be kept secret, for he was so touchy about money. I dare not upset him further, or hurt his feelings by earning money until he was settled in a job. Yet the need to express myself in some other medium than the purely physical sense was as urgent as ever.

Conversation with Paul was limited, and discussion usually centred on his prospects. Even his favourite operatic records failed to entertain him, and the only relaxation was to be found in the big bed, or the 'Adam and Eve'. My gay companion and dashing escort of the hostel had disappeared. How quickly he had succumbed to melancholy when the Fates rejected him. When his lively face lost its animation, it was heavy, pallid, unattractive. Yet as suddenly as he sank into the pit of despondency, he would emerge, smiling and boasting, when success tapped him on the shoulder.

This was my man – a Jekyll and Hyde character, comprising so many facets I was constantly alert to surprise and shock. The spoilt child was still there in the man of fifty. He could be kind and cruel, gentle and rough, angry and deeply contrite, but there was no warning, no indication what his mood would be at a certain hour of the day. When I expected rough treatment, I was surprised by gentleness. When I longed for sympathy, I was met by irritation. Because of his own robust health – Paul boasted he had never seen a doctor – I suffered the migraine attacks in silence, for there was no cure. But the 'headache' was always regarded with suspicion, when it coincided with his own plans to surprise me with an appetizing dish, or cooled his ardent passion!

'Not again!' he would groan, as I staggered upstairs to lie prostrate on the bed for another twenty-four hours. Then weak tears would wet my cheeks in weary self-pity – he doesn't love me – I wish I could die!

* * * * *

'Sweetheart! Come here a minute,' Paul called imperiously up the stairs one morning, and I hurried down to find him scanning a page of *The Times.*

'Read that,' he commanded, pointing out a small advertisement under a box number.

I read it aloud. ' "Personal assistant to Bond Street art dealer. Must be versatile, educated, willing to travel, languages useful, attractive remuneration." But darling, you know nothing about art, and it bores you,' I protested mildly.

'I could soon find out, and it wouldn't bore me if there was money to be made out of it.'

'That's true,' I agreed, for the eagerness in his voice was not to be discouraged. He had long since strayed into other fields of employment, and had applied for a variety of vacancies, including hotel management, catering, travel agents and couriers, as well as industry and commerce. 'After six months without a job, I would sell my soul to the Devil if he paid well!' This spark of the old vitality was good to see.

'Why not answer it now, and I will pop down to the village to post it, then it will get the ten o'clock collection?' I suggested.

'Good idea, my sweet,' he smiled, approvingly.

'I'll make more coffee.' I went to the kitchen to fill the kettle, but the water buckets were empty. Rubber boots and a mackintosh with a hood covered me completely as I went down the lane to the water tap. Neither the mud nor the dripping hedges depressed me, but the thought of London did. Paul had promised to keep away from London, and this was the first time he had replied to a London advertisement, but it had attracted him.

The quiet fields were sleeping, the naked branches of the trees black against the sullen sky. The cottage stood square and solid at the end of the path – a haven of peace against the troubled precariousness of the outside world. For if Paul was afraid of failure, I was afraid of malicious tongues.

'I won't go. I shall stay here. A woman must have a home.' I was talking aloud, as the bucket filled with water. If only I could be free to write all the week, and not have to watch the clock. Two of my short stories had been accepted for a woman's weekly periodical, but as the payment was on publication I was spared having to make an explanation, for it would be three months before I received the cheque, and by that time Paul would be working. Would he be proud or jealous of my small success? For the first time in my adult life I felt the need of a settled home, and the urge to write was so strong I was determined to dig in my heels and refuse to move. The rent was paid, and I had withdrawn ten pounds from my post office savings account in Worthing to pay for the coal and a ton of logs.

'They must wait for their money,' said Paul, carelessly, but bills worried me, and I was not anxious to add any further discredit to our dubious reputation in the village. I also paid the milkman and baker, for my small housekeeping allowance only covered the grocer and butcher, and I was too worried about Paul's bank balance to ask him for more.

Three days later, a reply by telegram invited Paul to telephone immediately. The telegram was signed with the two initials V.W.

'But I know this guy! He's an old business associate of pre-war days,' Paul told me, excitedly. 'There couldn't be two V.W.'s and he always signed his letters that way. He was in textiles, but he must have gone into the art business since the war. What a bit of luck to run into him again. He wouldn't have cabled, my sweet, if he didn't remember me.'

And he picked up the telephone to put through a call to London. Then he held out his hand to me, and I stood beside him while he waited for the connection.

'Sweetheart, this is it!' His eyes were shining, he kissed my mouth, but he was not thinking of me. I could feel his tense excitement in the grip of his hand, but it was not me exciting him, for when the voice answered, he dropped my hand, and forgot I was there.

Then I moved away and left him, with a strange feeling of desertion. Was this the man who would take Paul away from me, back to the big, busy world from which he came, I wondered. They were talking on the telephone for a full twenty minutes, and I was glad the call would be charged to the London number and not to us, for Paul was running up a heavy account with all his calls.

'Yes, it's the same guy, and I've got an appointment for tomorrow!'

I was snatched into his arms, and hugged exuberantly.

'Tell me about this V.W.'

I sat on the floor at his feet, and he talked over my head while I gazed into the bright flames darting up the chimney.

When he tilted my face and kissed me, it did not interrupt the story, and all the time I was wary of this man who called himself V.W. – for he was the first link with pre-war days that Paul had encountered in four and a half years.

'I've finished with that old world. It's a closed book. Forget it, my sweet,' he had told me. 'It wouldn't worry me if I never saw Manchester, London, New York or Paris again.'

Now the gleam of anticipation was back in his eyes, and his voice vibrated with excitement. Here was a man of the world, longing to be back in circulation. Today he would be my lover; tomorrow he would be gone, and I should be plunged into my first period of waiting – waiting for the 'phone to ring – waiting for a letter – waiting for him to come home.

'Where thou goest, I will go,' I had declared, vehemently. But now I was not going. I was staying here. And Paul had sworn that he was finished with the old life. But that was a year ago. We both had changed our minds, because circumstances had forced the change.

'What is he like, this V.W.?' I asked, suspiciously.

'He's a Polish Jew – short, stout, ugly as sin, but one of the shrewdest guys in the business – before the war. But he never mixed business with pleasure – too damn clever! He kept a mistress in those pre-war days, a lovely girl, young enough to be his daughter – Diane. They lived in one of the luxury flats on our block, in a residential suburb of Manchester, and Diane was one of the thirty unlucky residents who happened to be at home on the night of the raid. Poor old V.W. was badly shocked. Mind you, she was probably entertaining the current boyfriend at the time, for he gave her a lot of rope, providing she was there when he wanted her. Jacqueline and Diane were friends at one time, for they both were models at the same fashion house in Mayfair. I should say he was a man in his late fifties now. We used to meet in the bar at the "Grand" in the old days, when he wasn't away in Europe or the States.' Paul sighed nostalgically, but I was sick with apprehension, for the more he told me about V.W. the more I disliked him.

'You're very quiet, sweetheart?' said Paul, caressing me.

'I'm listening, darling.'

'What should I do without you?'

'You will manage, I expect, when the time comes.'

'What do you mean?'

'He may want you to go to the States, this V.W.?'

Then he was silent, but his hands gripped my breasts so tightly I winced with pain. We sat there, gazing at the uncertain future in the dancing flames. Early the next morning he left for London.

I had still to learn how to shut all thought of Paul out of my mind and concentrate on the writing, but now it was impossible. All thought and feeling followed him to London, and the imagination I should have been using on a story wandered away to the bar of the Cumberland Hotel, where they had arranged to meet, and to the two men greeting each other excitedly, then picking up the threads of six years, to close the gap on a long separation in a few short minutes. There would be a meal in the restaurant, prolonged indefinitely by a serious discussion on the appointment, for I was convinced that V.W. would look no further for an assistant when Paul walked back into his life. There was no need, for here was a man whose qualifications were known and proved, so the risk was negligible for V.W. and the proposition too attractive to resist.

'After six months without a job, I would sell my soul to the Devil if he paid me well!'

This was no idle boast, for Paul was desperate for a contract of employment before Christmas, only a month away, when all the extra expenses of the journey and presents for his wife and daughter had to be met. This time there would be no escape from the questions they would ask in ten days. Even Paul, with his plausible tongue, would find it difficult to invent a job, and describe prospects that were non-existent, under a barrage of questions from the woman and the girl! Restlessness, and a growing anxiety, drove me outdoors in the grey November mist, to walk to the village to post my own letters to Mother and my sister Mary, and buy more wool for the socks and gloves I was busily knitting for Christmas presents. My gifts were dull, and showed poor lack of originality, but I just hadn't the money to be more original, and even if I waited to do my shopping in Worthing, many of the gifts were still shoddy and expensive. Hand-knitted socks and gloves were expected from me, and once again I should hear the polite 'Thanks – jolly useful' from William, while my sisters-in-law assured me that hand-knitted gloves were exactly what they needed and so much warmer than leather.

A little family of six children with their faces pressed to the window of the sweet shop held my attention. Maternity had been satisfied for four years with all my 'boys' on Block Number Eight. It could never be satisfied completely, for I would have no child of my own. Could other women's children provide a substitute for my own, I wondered, as I watched the elder girl of the family sharing the sweets she had bought into eager, outstretched hands, and popping one quickly into the wide open mouth of the youngest, in a push-cart.

It was then that the idea of a club for children was born, and I wondered whether this particular little family would be allowed to join. Already I could foresee weeks of separation, when Paul was abroad on business, and I had to begin to organize my life afresh. I would have a dog for company on my long country walks, and children coming in on Saturdays to play games, paint, read comics, drink quantities of lemonade, and eat all the cakes I would bake! It would be fun, and I almost spent my precious shillings on comics and crayons, and put a notice in the shop window, there and then, but reminded myself I had still to hear from Paul about his plans, for it wouldn't do to have a flock of children swarming in the gate next Saturday afternoon if he was still in residence! But the idea had cheered me enormously, and my natural tendency to cheerfulness soon dispelled the early anxiety. Now I was more than ever determined to keep the cottage, and walked homewards with a light step, wondering how many mothers would allow their children to visit a 'fallen' woman? Paul had promised to 'phone me at seven o'clock, and I was winding the wool I had bought when the bell startled me.

'Hullo, sweetheart!'

It was the first time I had heard his voice on the 'phone. It was loud and clear, and I promptly answered, 'Hullo, darling!' then waited to hear his news. He wasted no time in idle chatter but plunged straight into business.

'Well, my sweet, V.W. has made me a very attractive offer.'

The excitement in his voice penetrated a mind made suddenly blunt with dismay. I had expected it, but I was still shocked.

'Then it's settled?' I asked tentatively.

'Well, V.W. wants it settled tonight. He's a darn impatient guy.'

'So are you,' I interrupted, and I heard his chuckle of amusement.

'As a matter of fact, I told him I had to think about it, and talk it over with you on the telephone. We are meeting for dinner at eight o'clock, and he will expect a definite answer then.'

'You want to accept, don't you?'

'Sure I do, sweetie. I am not likely to get another chance like this. I would be a fool to let it go, wouldn't I? Wouldn't I?' he persisted.

'You did promise to keep away from London.'

'Sweetheart, for God's sake be reasonable!'

Now I could hear the irritation in his voice.

'I've had no work for six months. Now this drops into my lap. It's fantastic! V.W. hasn't even seen any of the others, and he had over sixty replies to his advertisement. "You're the man I want, Paul," he told me. "Never mind you don't know a thing about art, that's a detail. You just follow me around for six months, and you'll be okay." So you see, my sweet, it all fits together like it was meant to happen. I should have to be on the spot, naturally, for much of the time would be spent in the showrooms in Bond Street when V.W. takes a trip over to the Continent.' He paused, waiting for me to answer.

'I am staying here, Paul. I am not moving.'

He must have heard the tremor in my voice, for now I was crying.

'Sweetheart, I must go – that appointment was fixed for eight o'clock, and I have to get to the "Caprice" in Piccadilly. I will ring back tomorrow night at the same time. Keep your fingers crossed for me!'

'I will say a little prayer for you,' I answered automatically. Then the receiver clicked, and soon he would be swallowed up in the swirl of traffic in Piccadilly, and be marching boldly into a crowded restaurant, immaculate in a Savile Row suit and spotted bow tie – while I sat alone, hunched on the sagging old sofa, weeping for a man already lost to this quiet backwater of Somerset – lost because he had never really belonged to it, and only suffered it for my sake. Those 'small inconveniences' were madly irritating to Paul. I had been too impulsive again, and second thoughts would have shown me a more sensible solution to the problem of accommodation before we left the hostel.

Now my determination was weakening at the prospect of separation. How could I bear to have Paul living in London, if I stayed in Somerset? Could writing, or children, or dogs, compensate for the company of this one dearly-loved man, I asked myself, as I climbed the stairs to my big, lonely bed.

But he didn't 'phone the following evening, and I was left in no doubt that he was already so immersed in the new challenging world of Bond Street, he could spare no time for me. I had disappointed him. When he expected enthusiasm, I had shown only a mild interest, and a reluctance to accept the sensible conclusion that London was the centre for enterprising men, while this cottage was merely a haven into which one crept at old age. This, to Paul, was so obvious, I was sure he had expected me to pack my bags, hand over the key, and catch the first train to London.

Now I could settle to nothing at all, and by nine o'clock my nerves were ragged with waiting for the 'phone to ring. I was hearing tinkling bells all the time, and rushing to pick up the receiver. Every sound was magnified by fear and anxiety. A hot cinder dropping in the hearth made me jump with fright, and the silence was awful since I switched off the radio when I expected the call. I had eaten nothing but bread and butter all day, and made a dozen pots of tea. The hours dragged by. Should I ring the hotel? He would be so annoyed if he was in conference with V.W.

For the second night I crept upstairs with a candle, and the shadows on the wall I never noticed when Paul was there, were big and menacing. Worn out with crying, I fell asleep at last, and was rudely awakened by a loud banging on the front door, and a beam of light on the window. I lit the candle and went downstairs, shivering and dazed, and pulled back the heavy bolt.

Paul was standing on the threshold, and I stared stupidly as though I had seen a ghost. He took the candle from my trembling hand, and put it carefully down on the table. Then he folded his arms around me, and I clung to him, laughing and crying.

'How come you go to bed before I get home?' he demanded.

'I thought – I thought . . .' I stuttered.

'You thought I was not coming back? I heard it in your

voice last night, and you were crying. Do you realize what you've done?'

I shook my head, and stroked his cold face.

'I have just turned down a job worth a thousand a year, and I reckon I'm a bloody fool! Now I'm starved, for I've had nothing to eat all day. And where's the coffee?'

I threw some sticks on to the dying embers. I was still in my nightdress, still dazed and shivering.

'Food? Coffee?' I echoed, stumbling towards the kitchen. Then he laughed, and wrapped me round in his overcoat.

'I was only kidding, sweetheart! Kiss me! I can wait,' he said.

'A man must work or lose his dignity,' Paul told me as he lay beside me, relaxed and mollified, in the big bed.

I had given all of myself, and taken all, without reservation. Released from an agonizing decision and doubting his own ability to decide for the best, he came back to me in a state of nervous exhaustion, for in doing something so against his will and inclination, he was also being unfair to himself. Every natural impulse had been beaten into a self denial that was completely alien to his nature. It would be a long time before he could forgive me the strange hold I had over him. It was not only a physical hold, but something more, an indefinable sense of belonging, of deep attachment, of knowing and caring, believing and trusting; he was more vulnerable than I thought him to be, and I was both proud and ashamed that the urge to come back to me was so strong in the midst of so much persuasion. It was, for me, the biggest surprise in all the time I had known him. It was also an added responsibility, for now he blamed me for losing an opportunity not likely to come his way again. He would be difficult to live with until he found another post - difficult and demanding. All my tact and tolerance would not compensate for this second vital decision in my favour in one year. He was angry with me, because he had allowed himself to surrender a little of his proud, dominating personality to me, a woman. He was rough with me, because, in a weak moment, he had been too gentle.

For several weeks I was a slave to his every whim, and all thought of writing stories, starting a club for children, or buying a dog, was dismissed from my mind. I did not dare to question him about V.W. or what had actually happened.

Then, one evening, he wound up the gramophone, and put on a record of mine – *The Warsaw Concerto* – one I had played so often at the hostel. Paul called it my signature tune. He pulled me on his knees and said, 'That finished it for me. I was walking along the pavement in Piccadilly, and a small little guy with a monkey was playing this tune on a barrel organ. I walked past, then went back and dropped half-a-crown in his hat. "Thank you, sir," he said, and beamed at me like he was surprised to see a coin that big. "Thank *you*, my friend, for reminding me of someone," I told him. But he just grinned. Maybe he couldn't speak English, only "thank you". Maybe he thought I was crazy. He could be right!'

'Oh, my darling, it was a lovely gesture.' I kissed him gratefully. But he was still frowning, still troubled by a gesture he could not understand. In retrospect, I still wonder whether he should have made it, for the pattern of our lives would have been drastically changed had he accepted the post of assistant to V.W. – changed for the better, perhaps, since it could hardly work out worse? What next,' I wondered.

One evening, in mid-December, he went off to the 'Adam and Eve' as usual, after the six o'clock news, and by eleven o'clock he was not back. He had never been later than nine, and sometimes he stayed for barely an hour, depending on his mood and the customers. The supper I had prepared was ruined, and I sat there, piling coal on the fire, drinking tea to keep myself awake, busy with the last pair of socks for Christmas. He could have 'phoned, but he hadn't. What had happened now? Would he surprise me again in a different way, in this aggressive mood? Because we loved so intensely, we suffered. We could hurt each other far more than any outside influence. This vulnerability that love had brought touched my every word and thought when Paul was with me. Our separateness had diminished, and I was not even sure that I could write, or wanted to write, another story. Since his return from London, I had done no more than write a few letters and Christmas cards.

Once again the silence was oppressive, the clock ticked loudly – half-past eleven, twelve o'clock, half-past twelve – but this time I was determined to be awake when he returned – *if* he returned. Alert now to every sound, I heard the hurrying footsteps coming down the lane, and flung open the door with a pounding heart.

'Paul! Darling! I thought you had changed your mind and gone back to London. You are so unpredictable, I am never sure.'

He was waving a bunch of holly.

'Happy Christmas from Mabel!' he shouted.

I could smell whisky on his breath, and burst into tears.

'Sweetheart, don't cry. It's *all right!*' he told me excitedly. 'I've got myself a marvellous job, almost on the doorstep – well, only thirty miles from here. Would you believe it? I've been appointed Catering Officer at the American Base, with a starting salary of seven-fifty, increased to a thousand in six months, if my services are satisfactory. The appointment dates from January 1st, the day after I get back from Ireland. Kiss me! For God's sake, my sweet! I feel like I've just been handed a million dollars!'

'Darling, you're wonderful! I'm so proud of you.'

I dragged him in and bolted the door, and he hugged me exuberantly.

'Do you want to eat? The supper's ruined hours ago, but I could make another.'

'Let's both eat. I'll bet you've had nothing but cups of tea all evening!' he teased me. 'You make the coffee and I'll make the omelettes. Is that the time? It can't be. My poor sweetheart, no wonder you were worried.'

And he tossed his hat and overcoat on a chair, and strode into the kitchen.

'You must tell me everything from start to finish when we've had our supper – or is it breakfast we are having?' I giggled.

'Kiss me!' he said – 'again, with feeling. That's better.'

He was beating eggs in a basin, his lips pursed, his eyes bright with fun. The transformation was incredible. His face was lit like the lamp in the window. He was the same man who walked towards the Block, swinging his heavy bags in May, 1942. The old disarming grin was back.

'I want to do three things at once – cook the omelettes, talk my head off, and make love to you!' he laughed excitedly, threw a lump of butter in the pan, and poured in the eggs. In ten minutes we had finished the meal, and he was sitting on the sofa sipping black coffee, while I knelt between his knees, adoring him with my eyes. A Catering Officer? Why not? There was nothing he couldn't do if he set his mind to it.

'What I can do you can do,' V.W. had told him. And for all I knew he was already planning the menu for January first!

'Sit over there, my sweet. You make me nervous when you look at me like I was a big ham!' He pushed me away.

'You are a big ham!'

I sat back in my chair with my feet on the fender, as wide awake now as at any time during the day. 'I'm listening. Start at the beginning.'

'Okay – It was George and Mabel who put me on to it,' he began. 'As soon as I showed my face in the bar, George called out, "Ah, Mr Taylor, just the man we want to see, eh, Mabel?" Now Mabel was up on the counter, decorating a portrait of the Queen with paper roses, so I had to admire her handiwork before she could put her mind to anything else. "She's luvly, isn't she?" she said, and I agreed the Queen was lovely, and helped her down off the counter. "Two American chaps have been asking for you. Came in this morning and coming again tonight," she told me. "Why, what have I done?" I laughed. Then George cut in. "Oh, you've not done nothing as we know of, Mr Taylor. It was a proposition they had to make." "A proposition?" My ears were flapping, sweetie. "What else did they say?" I asked Mabel. "Something about a job at the Base," she said, and poured me a drink. *"Say that again!"* I yelled at her, and she laughed her head off, and said I was a real caution.'

'So you are, my love. Go on, what then?' I interrupted, for I was not very interested in George and Mabel since I was not likely to meet them. He stretched himself on the sofa, lit a cigarette and went on with the story.

The two Americans had come back to the 'Adam and Eve' soon after eight o'clock, and introduced themselves to Paul. They had heard about his wartime activities at 'The Plough' and had traced him to the 'Adam and Eve' because they seemed to consider he was a suitable candidate for the vacancy at the Base. In the past two years they had had seven Catering Officers, apparently, and 'couldn't figure out why the guys kept leaving'. So Captain Kemsley put his proposition to Paul, while Lieutenant Parker collected the drinks and brought them to a table away from the rest of the customers. Then they all went off in a jeep to the Base, where he was questioned for an hour or more by a Major Robert S. Martin, while they smoked American cigarettes and drank American coffee.

'It was a kind of security screening, like we had during the war,' Paul explained. 'Why did I take a post with the Westhill Aircraft Company? Was there a motive behind it? Had I any ideas on Communism? And where were my parents raised? All that sort of thing. I got a bit hot under the collar when we got round to questions about the family.'

He looked at me fondly, and added, 'You are my wife, and don't you forget it, if anyone checks on me.'

'I'll try not,' I promised, but now I was worried again.

'By the time the Major had finished with me, I was ready for a drink, then he showed me round the department I shall be responsible for. He has to check on my credentials, of course, but it's only a formality, and he seemed satisfied. Anyway, he fixed a date for starting, and transport will be arranged. An Army Corporal will pick me up in a jeep at half-past seven in the morning, and bring me back in the evening, and I'm to have a free hand in engaging local staff – all females, by the way!' he grinned, and yawned expansively. 'Come to bed, my sweet. I guess the rest of the details will keep till tomorrow!'

It seemed too good to be true. After eight long months Paul was actually on his way to work, and I was being kissed goodbye on the threshold, like a million other wives, at seven-thirty on the 1st of January, 1947. His kiss, too, was like a million others, absent-minded, impatient to be off, and his lips brushed mine without feeling or emotion. He was ready on the stroke of seven-thirty, alert and spruce in a heavy dark overcoat, the homburg hat and a new pair of gloves from Rosalinde.

'Aren't they beautiful? She saved up her pocket money to buy them,' he had told me proudly on his return from Ireland the day before. But now we both would be forgotten all day – the child and I – and the doors firmly closed on the separate little compartments reserved for us in his heart.

A dark shape emerged from the shadows and a voice, with a strong American flavour, called cheerfully, 'Ready when you are, sir.'

'So long, sweetheart.' He lifted a hand in salute, then he was gone, and I heard the screech of brakes at the sharp bend in the road.

'Thank God!' I breathed gratefully. The relief was so tremendous, I found my eyes were wet, and my whole body weak and limp. I had been down early to light the lamp and the fire, and to make coffee for Paul and tea for myself. Our little sitting-room was a bright, cheerful place on this dark Winter morning. Now I could make toast and have a leisurely breakfast, do my few chores, and have a long day at the writing.

During the Christmas holiday, away from Paul, under the calm influence of Mother, I had regained my independent thought, and myself as a separate entity. It was good to be starting a new challenging chapter on the first day of the New Year, good to feel the old urge to start on a new story. For I also had ambition - an ambition that was separate from Paul and concerned only that part of me he could never reach. I was surprised to find it was still there, waiting in my subconscious mind - waiting for Paul to start work, to leave me alone all day, six days a week.

'You mustn't get worried about me if I don't show up till after eight o'clock, for I shall want to check that everything is okay before I leave,' he had told me, as he brushed his sparse grey hair. 'It's a hell of a long day for you, sweetheart, especially in the Winter, but at least you know I shall be coming home every night like a good husband!' he had flung at me, as he gulped hot coffee. And I sighed with happiness, helped him into his overcoat, and handed him hat, gloves, and briefcase.

'So long, sweetheart.'

'Goodbye, my darling. Have a good day.'

The echo of his voice was still here, and the room vibrated with his strong personality. When the daylight filtered through the window, I would open the door to let in a current of cold, frosty air. Then he would be gone, and I should be alone all day. I had to be alone sometimes, but he must never know that I felt this way, for he would be jealous of the time spent in this small, secret world of creation. Perhaps a child would have satisfied this deep urge to create, but then the child, grown strong with independent life, would leave me, as I had left my own mother. Mine was a small talent, but it was at least a gift of God, for it hadn't been given to me by past or present relationship. Talents were distributed among the family, but there had never been a writer of stories - only letters and diaries. Now I knew exactly what form the story would take, I was anxious to start on it, and even the hour spent on chores that first morning seemed tedious. There had been time enough during the ten days in Worthing to make a list of chapter headings, for this would be a book for children – little girls – based on the Bible story of Ruth, and I had spent hours in the Public Library, studying maps, and browsing over old books.

With chapter headings I had no need of notes, for I knew I had only to read about the childhood of Ruth to see her as a child with her parents, brothers and sisters and friends – to hear her speak, to know her thoughts – always of a serious nature. never flippant. I could describe her eyes and hair, her dress, and the way she climbed the hill. The picture would be there in my mind, but I had to take one step at a time, for to look ahead at the second chapter heading would confuse me. This had been made clear to me from the age of about seven or eight, at the village school, when a lackadaisical school teacher, wishing to enjoy a respite from the three 'R's', would pick on a subject – an animal in a picture on the wall, a child in class, or even an object like a desk. Pointing a finger, she would command, 'Write me a story about that!' While the rest of the class sucked their pencils, I was absorbed and happy, filling two pages of the exercise book with sprawling, untidy writing, and coming to an abrupt halt when the teacher cried, 'Stop!'

Now, with my feet on the fender, and a pad on my knees, I began to write, and the hours passed so swiftly I was surprised to find it was already mid-day. Yet I had written only a few pages, and my pen had moved slowly and laboriously, not flowing easily, as I had expected. It was there, inside me, but couldn't get out. I was exhausted, my mind a blank, as I went to the kitchen to make a sandwich and a cup of tea. It was disappointing, but I told myself I should do better to-morrow, be more fluent. It was too soon, and my body was still tired after last night's excited love-making. Emotions had been spent in physical satisfaction, and all my senses used, but this one small, secret sense of creativity, too long stifled by these months of waiting and anxiety. There must be release now from these constant demands, from a sensuality that was becoming too demanding and too important. Love was not only sexual intercourse, and a satisfying of the body's urgent demands; it must be more discriminating in future. 'Not to-night, my love,' must be told more firmly, and I must not be weakened by that hard mouth, or that twisting tongue, or those big, caressing hands! Now that Paul had regained his manhood in work, he had no need to be reassured so often, to drain me dry of emotion and feeling that I now had to use, for a time, in my own way.

'Not to-night, my love.' Would he be surprised? Would he be angry? But no, he was only amused.

'Sweetheart, where do you find all this determination? How come you can resist such an ardent Romeo!' Then he flung an arm over me and slept like a babe till morning!

He came back boastful and confident that first day, soon after eight o'clock.

'Sweetheart, it was marvellous! The pace is terrific! I haven't stopped a second all day,' he told me excitedly.

'No meals, no coffee?'

'Standing up – no time to sit – I had a steak brought to my office at two o'clock, but there were so many interruptions I never got around to finishing it. But plenty of strong, black coffee, and a double whisky on the way back at a nice little pub called the "Fox and Hounds". Boy! What a day!' he laughed, and spread his arms, and I went into them. He held me close for a long moment. 'Could I take a bath, sweetie? I feel sort of stale with all that food cooking all day.'

'What food?'

'Steaks, hamburgers, fried eggs and ham. Those guys never stop eating. And would you believe it, they bring their wives and kids to the canteen – babies in high chairs and kids all over the place. You never heard such a racket. They all drink milk, gallons of milk, and gallons of ice-cream.'

'You mean, the men drink milk as well as the children?'

'Sure, they drink plenty.'

'Darling, you come home, after one day at the Base, one hundred per cent American!' I teased him. 'But don't start calling me "Honey" or chewing gum – I'm warning you!'

Then I hurried down the lane with a torch and two buckets, to fill the copper, while he glanced through the morning paper. I had tramped for several miles along the frosted lanes in the afternoon, and came back hungry for tea. Now I was glad to have Paul back, and ready to listen again, for he would want to tell me everything that had happened. Then he would say, as an afterthought, 'And what have you been doing with yourself all day, my sweet?'

But my vague answer would not bother him, and there would be no probing enquiries as to how I spent my time.

'I must tell you about Doris and Ada,' he began – putting down the paper, and lighting another cigarette. 'They do all the washing up, by machine, of course, for that's the American way. All the equipment is shipped over from the States, even a machine for making doughnuts. Now I knew about these two dames, for the Major had given me a list of my staff with all their various jobs.'

'Women,' I corrected, firmly, 'not dames.'

He grinned and went on, 'These two women were standing in the door of my office when I arrived. I felt a bit annoyed, but it wouldn't do to show it. Got to be a diplomat now, my sweet, as well as a Catering Officer. "We've come to 'and in our notice, me and Ada," said Doris decidedly. Then I knew my troubles had started, for the Major had warned me that only these two older women would stay on the washing up machines, all the younger ones want to work in the canteen, where they can be seen. "There are only two reasons that I know of, Taylor, for working at the American base – we pay well, and all these dames see themselves as G.I. brides!" he told me. I laughed at that, but it so happened the Major was right.'

'What did you do with Doris and Ada?' I asked curiously.

'Made love to 'em – with cups of tea, and compliments!'

'And are they still there?'

'At the moment. Doris is considering the matter for a week.'

'And Ada?'

'She's just a poor stooge. Doris is the boss.'

'What was the trouble?'

'Too much interference, too many guys walking around on tours of inspection. It's got to stop. I won't have my staff upset – and I'm not licking the Major's boots, either!'

'You might give me a hand with this bath water – Big-head!' I reminded him.

But I could understand the position by Paul's dramatic imitations, and his talent for mimicry, given full play with characters like Doris and Ada, the cheeky youngsters in the canteen who called him 'Boss', and the curt Major, kept me laughing that first evening. And I loved the way he referred to *my* staff, *my* girls, *my* department, as though he had been there for years.

'Those other guys must have been licking the Major's boots, my sweet, for he seemed a bit surprised to have somebody standing up to him. Although I had his sanction to engage staff, my authority ended there, and any fool guy of a deputy could come around looking for a speck of dust in the kitchens and canteen. *Hygiene,* that's the Major's baby. He's crazy about hygiene, and you can imagine how our Doris reacts to the word,' he chuckled. 'She doesn't even know what it means, for a start. "What's all this blarney about eyegeen, Sir? I never 'eard tell of it till I come to this place," she told me. "Couldn't even get a blinkin' tea cloth for drying up our cups and saucers after our elevenses, so I brought one from 'ome. 'Oo does 'e think 'e is, anyway, this Major Martin - God Almighty? I give 'im a bit of my tongue, I don't mind tellin' you, sir, when they come snooping round my department. You can't tell me nothin' about washing up I don't know already. I been at it long before your Mum was changing your nappy! I told the last one." Then she laughed her head off. She's a great character.'

'They're the salt of the earth, those older country women. You hang on to them if you can,' I told Paul.

'I intend to, for the young ones come and go all the time apparently, and you can't depend on them. There is always somebody waiting to step into the shoes of Maureen, or Deirdre, or Carole, but nobody wants Doris's job. They give their girls some fancy names, these old-fashioned Mums. I've even got a Felicity and a Penelope, but I notice they get called Cissy and Penny. Two older women clean the canteen twice a day - Gertie and Grace - on their hands and knees, mark you. So I intend to look after these four, I can't afford to lose them.' He frowned, tossed a stub of cigarette into the fire, and lit another. He seemed very tense and nervous, I thought, but the bath relaxed him, and when he stretched on the sofa, in a warm dressing gown and slippers, he sighed with relief and smiled at me.

'It was just what I needed, sweetheart. I was getting stale. Responsibility and plenty of work, I thrive on it. Though I'm not so keen on the paper work, with every darn thing in triplicate. Nearly as bad as the Civil Service! "Give me a free hand, Major, for three months," I told him, before I left this evening, "then, if I make a mess of it, you can sack me!" '

My heart plunged. 'Darling, must you be quite so blunt? He

may take you at your word.'

'Don't you worry. I've got him nicely sized up, and I know how far I can go without putting my foot in it. I reckon he likes a bit of opposition, for it gives him a chance to argue. A "yes" man would bore him. He's a bit of a tough guy, with a jutting jaw – reminds me of Spencer Tracy.'

'Then for heaven's sake be careful,' I warned.

'It's marvellous to feel on top of the world again, not grovelling about at the bottom,' he said, as we went upstairs – 'and I'm as strong as a lion, so the pace won't break me!' he added, with the old, boastful arrogance.

The pattern of my days had changed again, and in some ways I was disappointed by the change. The old gregarious appetite for company, for an audience, for the sound of his own voice, was stronger than the urge to come home at the end of the day.

'Sweetheart, I need to unwind, and an hour or so in that little pub puts me in a good mood. It's the pressure, it's terrific. You've no idea, and all those guys are so *young*,' he explained.

I sighed. Why couldn't he come home to unwind? I begrudged the time he spent in the 'Fox and Hounds', for soon it was extended to a couple of hours, and a new anxiety crept into my waiting – was he drinking too much?

'You will never see me drunk, my sweet – maybe a bit intoxicated, but not drunk,' he had promised me, when I shuddered at the smell of whisky on his breath one night. I pulled a face, and turned my head away, and refused his kiss. Then I saw his eyes were wet when I served his supper, and I was ashamed to be so fastidious.

'Darling, I'm sorry. I'll get used to it,' I told him contritely.

'Will you kiss me now? – I guess I can't stand you being cross with me,' he pleaded.

Arrogance and humility – what a strange mixture of temperament he could provide in one short evening, this man of mine, I thought. At such moments as this, my love was maternal. I felt old and wise – so much older and wiser than Paul. And the writing had given me a new confidence that was lacking before. In three months, the story of Ruth had taken shape and grown in my mind, like a child in the womb. It was, for me, as real and substantial as any child, having life and meaning in its concept and growth. Every sentence of every page had been drawn, not from memory, but imagination. Yet it was not a fantasy or a parody on the Bible story. It had occupied my mind through the long days of Winter, while the wind howled and the snow drifted over fields and garden. With a stiff yard broom I swept the snow away, and poured kettles of boiling water over the frozen tap.

'Just another small inconvenience, sweetie?' asked Paul, hurrying past to curl his big, heavy body into the small seat of the jeep. But I laughed at him, and went on sweeping, for the weather was the least of my worries.

'This is nothing. We had six weeks of snow in Kent every Winter, and snowploughs to clear a path through the village so that we could get to school!' I boasted.

Paul looked at me, and shivered.

Then the first snowdrops appeared, hanging their drooping white heads on stems so slender it seemed they must break at every puff of wind.

'Darling! Snowdrops!' I yelled excitedly, one morning, as I hurried back up the path.

Paul was standing with his hands to the fire, warming himself, waiting for his driver.

'Did you notice them under the pear tree when you went down the garden?'

'It was too darn cold to mess around. If we have to spend another Winter here, I'm having an inside loo and bathroom.'

'Come and look at them, *please?'* I urged, ignoring his good intentions for extra comfort. It would be too expensive, and we could never afford it. Besides, we were only renting the cottage.

'You're crazy,' he grumbled, but followed me down the path, barely glancing at the tiny heralds of Spring. 'They are such small little flowers, I could pass them a dozen times and not see them.'

'That's why they are so special.'

'I guess you're right, but I can't feel the way you do about flowers – there's Butch hooting. I must go. So long, sweetheart.' He brushed my lips and hurried away – a man of action, with no time to stand and stare!

'Don't be too late back, to-night,' I called after him.

'Okay,' he answered, absent mindedly.

Everything was okay now.

I was surprised and confused when Paul arrived home one night with the two Army sergeants who often accompanied him to the little wayside pub, and went back in the jeep. I had heard about Gary and Bob, but hadn't expected to meet them.

They stood together in the tiny porch, three big men, wearing big smiles. The American boys had been promised a warm welcome, but seemed a little uncertain now that they were actually on the doorstep, and I was too surprised to greet them. It was after ten o'clock, and Paul had 'phoned me at eight to say he was on the way, and would I have something ready in the oven because he was starving. With all that food around the Base? Apparently he lost his appetite all day and found it again when he arrived home. It was irritating to think of all those steaks and hamburgers, fried eggs and ham, in vast quantities, while I still had to provide him with supper. But Paul was not capable of such reasoning, and since he had increased my housekeeping allowance, I had no cause to complain. (I was paying a typist to type my manuscript, and consequently a little mean with the groceries!)

Tonight I was faced with two strangers for the first time on the threshold of our home – a home I had hoped to be safe from strangers who would ask too many questions.

'How do, Ma'am,' they chorused, holding out their big hands to me.

'I hope we don't intrude, Ma'am, but your husband said to come right along,' Gary explained.

Paul stepped inside, beaming affably at my blank face.

'Isn't she marvellous?' he demanded, and squeezed my shoulder affectionately. 'Come on in, boys, make yourselves at home, and my wife will make us some coffee – the American way. She's a champion coffee-maker, and a first-rate cook.'

'That's not true.' I found my voice at last. 'I am a very poor cook. Paul is the cook when he's at home on Sunday.'

'She gets her breakfast in bed. How's that for spoiling? You two guys make a note of that. You can't go wrong if you give your wives their breakfast in bed on Sunday morning!'

Gary and Bob laughed politely, and sat down awkwardly on the old sofa, stretching their long legs to the blazing fire.

'Gee, this is real cosy. I reckon it's the first fire I've seen since I left home, and that was three years last fall,' said Gary.

'It sure is homey, Ma'am,' Bob agreed, with a slow smile.

They were grown men with the faces of young boys, and

close cropped heads. Their uniforms fitted so tightly I expected to hear the seams ripping as they sat down, and their hands were big and clumsy on the dainty china – Mother had spared me six cups and saucers from her china cabinet. And they both were so inarticulate, I could only suppose that Paul had deliberately selected these two from the crowd to accompany him to the little pub at the end of the day. Paul wanted an audience, not competition!

So he sat there at ease, in the only decent armchair – we had bought it second-hand at a local sale – smoking, talking, drinking coffee, while I found my attention wandering, and my eyelids closing. So much of my own nervous energy was expounded in my writing now, but Paul, supposing I had a very easy day, naturally expected me to be lively and interested late at night!

'Then you had no children, Ma'am?'

My eyes snapped open. I could feel my cheeks burning in the firelight.

'Unfortunately no,' I told Gary, and Paul added nothing to a subject on which I dare not experiment.

'Your husband tells me you did a lot of travelling before the war, before your marriage. That's very interesting, Ma'am,' said Bob, shyly.

Obviously they were trying to draw me into a conversation that was nothing more than a monologue, so I had no choice but to muster my reluctant senses, and play the hostess, with a few amusing anecdotes of Bombay and Karachi, and my early adventures as a children's nurse on board ship. Paul laughed as readily as the two American boys, encouraging me to talk of my travels. Once the dangerous topic of marriage was averted, I was less nervous of contradicting something Paul had already told them.

At half past eleven, Gary looked at his watch, and exclaimed, 'Gee! We must get cracking, Bob, or we shan't be back at Base before twelve.'

They shook hands and thanked me profusely for my kind hospitality, and ran off down the lane like two schoolboys. Still smiling and pleased, Paul bolted the door and took me in his arms.

'Paul, please *must* we entertain? Don't you see enough of them all day? It makes me nervous. I was so afraid of embarrassing you with some stupid mistake.'

'You could never embarrass me, my sweet, for I don't know the meaning of the word. Surely you know me better. You were marvellous. Anyway, I don't know why you worry, for I would always cover up for you if you came unstuck.'

'But I don't *want* them!' I wailed – and burst into tears.

'Well, if you're going to get upset every time I bring my friends home, I guess I'll do my entertaining some place else in future,' he told me, suddenly deflated – and sat back on the sofa to light another cigarette.

I sat down in the opposite corner, not touching, not even wanting to touch him, and closed my wet eyes. Paul made no attempt to comfort me. I slept exhausted. We both slept.

At two o'clock I awoke, stiff with cramp, in Paul's arms.

'Wake up, woman!' he yelled. 'I'm starving!'

'Are you, darling? What would you like to eat – shall I warm up the stew?' I asked him, with a mighty yawn.

And I did not see Gary and Bob again.

* * * * *

This chapter at the American Base lasted for a little over three years, and I was surprised it lasted so long, with all the pressure from headquarters, staff troubles, and the Major's fanatical concern with hygiene! During that period, I found contentment in my own absorbing interests – writing, gardening, the joy of a real home, and the children.

Only on Saturdays when Paul was at work was the peace disturbed by the children. I began to collect them in the February of that eventful year – 1947. 'Collect' is the only word to describe the gradual trickle of curious children pushing open the gate, peering through the hedges, and climbing over the fence. They came cautiously, and there was no rush to join my Saturday Club for Children (aged four to eleven years) advertised in the Post Office. Country children are usually cautious, and their busy Mums, anxious to get them out of the way on Saturdays, seemed slow to decide whether I was a respectable woman.

I was delighted to find the little family I had once encountered at the sweet shop were the first to venture down our lane, to bang with their fists on the front door. They stood in the porch, gazing up at me with their solemn faces.

' 'ullo,' said the eldest. 'We've come.'

'Hullo,' I said. 'That's fine – and you've brought the baby?'

'Mum said we 'ad to bring 'im else we couldn't come.'

'I see. How old is he?' I asked, dubiously, for I was not prepared for toddlers.

'Three on the 23rd of March. We always take 'im with us in the push cart and 'e's no bother.'

'Well, come on in, all of you, and you must tell me your names.'

She picked up the youngest, took a deep breath and recited, – 'Connie – Bertie – Emmie – Jackie – the baby's Willy and I'm Rose.'

They all trooped in to my small sitting-room.

'It's nice,' said Rose, her sharp eyes darting over the bright new matting, the bowl of anemones on the window sill, and the blazing fire. The big polished table was spread with card games, jigsaw puzzles, paints, crayons, drawing-books and comics. The two boys pounced on the comics and fell on the sofa. Connie wandered into the kitchen to inspect the jug of lemonade, buns and biscuits, Emmie into the garden, and Rose stood on the hearth rug with Willy astride her hip, and looked me over carefully. Then a slow smile crept over her anxious little face, and she tucked a strand of lank hair behind her ear.

'Nobody never thought of it before, only you. It's a good idea to 'ave a club, makes a nice change.'

And she put the heavy child on to a chair with a sigh of relief, called the two girls sharply to the table, and sat down between them.

'Shall we 'ave "Ludo" first, or "Snakes and Ladders"?'

' "Snap"!' said Connie, picking up the new packet.

'Trust you to be awkward!' said Rose fiercely, but dealt out the cards.

Willy, kneeling on the chair, grabbed at the cards, and Emmie sighed, 'Oh dear, now 'e wants to play.'

'Well, let 'im,' said Rose, sensibly, and gave him extra cards to keep him quiet.

It was all so quickly organized, and taken so completely out of my hands, I could only stand and watch admiringly. The next to arrive, at the back door, was a girl of about eight or nine with red-gold hair and very blue eyes, and Rose looked up from her cards to say, carelessly, 'Oh, it's Brenda Jackson. Thought you said you wasn't coming?'

'Can if I like!' Brenda retorted, and stepped inside.

'Hullo, Brenda. How nice of you to come. What would you

like to do?' I waved a hand invitingly over the table, where Rose had stacked it all in a neat pile.

'Draw,' she said.

'That's all she thinks about – *drawing*,' Rose jeered.

'Well, and why not? It's a very good hobby' – and I handed out a drawing book and crayons.

'I only draw with a pencil, crayons are for little children,' Brenda reminded me, so I had to search for a pencil among my own writing materials.

'Thanks,' she said, and lay on her stomach, flat on the hearth rug, and began to draw a horse. Shouts of 'Snap!' and the rustle of comics on the sofa was the only indication that I had already seven children in my sitting-room. Then, some time later, two small boys climbed over the fence from the fields, and dropped into a bed of wall-flowers I had planted in the Autumn. They were typical urchins of seven or eight, grubby, untidy, and ready for mischief. I had only to look at them to know they would not fit in anywhere – no games, or drawing or even comics, would keep these two bright lads amused. They tumbled in the door, and stood there, hands in pockets, grinning impishly at the other children.

'Oh, lord, it's them!' groaned Rose, scooping all the cards into her lap.

Brenda merely glanced up and went on drawing.

'Well, two more recruits! That's fine. That makes nine,' I told them heartily, and they rocked with laughter, as though it was all unaccountably funny. 'Well, it's half-past ten, so you are just in time for elevenses,' – and again they yelled at me, pushing each other around. 'Come into the kitchen, you two boys. It's getting a bit crowded in here.'

I had no idea what I was going to do with them. What did one do with two lively small boys on a Saturday morning in February? I wondered, as I handed round glasses of lemonade, buns and biscuits.

Rose took a bib from her pocket and tied it round Willy's neck, and her eyes darted over the rest of the family. When Bertie slyly took two chocolate biscuits off the plate, she jumped up, slapped his hand, and reminded him sharply, 'Be'ave yourself now, or you won't come no more!'

Brenda went on drawing, with lemonade and biscuits on the fender beside her. The boys told me their names were Peter and Michael, and they lived next door to each other. When they had finished up the buns that were left over, I was still undecided what to do with them, but apparently they had already decided it would be more fun in the woodshed. They ran off, hooting and happy, but appeared five minutes later with the tatty remains of an old pram the last tenants had left behind, and I hadn't the heart to get rid of it, for once it had been modelled on exactly the same lines as the pram that had carried our two youngest to the hop-gardens in Kent, with a deep well in the middle for feet and parcels. I had forgotten it was still there, but the boys had dragged it out, covered in dust and rust, minus a hood, and with several broken spokes, as though they had discovered a priceless treasure.

'Can we borrow it, miss? We won't break it,' Michael told me.

'And we'll put it back when we've finished with it, ready for next time,' said Peter.

For the next hour or so they dashed up and down the lane, taking turns to ride. The problem of Peter and Michael had solved itself, and they came every week to push each other around in the pram, and for no other reason.

But now it was Spring, and the children were home for the Easter holidays. Paul went to Ireland, and I went to Worthing as usual, but when I came back, I posted another notice on the board, announcing a picnic to Poacher's Wood the following Saturday, and added, 'PLEASE BRING FOOD'. They swarmed down the lane at ten o'clock – nearly thirty children, and some of them strangers – friends and relatives of the twenty odd children now attached to the Saturday Club. (I had divided them into two age groups, for morning and afternoon.)

Now I felt like Mother Hubbard, as I sorted them out, and asked, 'Have you all got food?'

'Yes,' they chorused, but then I discovered some had only a slice of bread and jam in a paper bag, or one meat sandwich to last all day. Prepared for an invasion, I had packed several bags with bread, butter, potted meat, sausages, potatoes, a kettle, an old frying-pan, tea, sugar and milk, several tin plates and mugs, and a small first-aid kit!

We set off, with my two young urchins heading the procession with the old pram, packed with all our equipment. Rose had Willy in the pushcart, and two of the children had brought dogs.

I laugh at the memory still – the children straggling along

the lanes, and two little sisters, hand in hand, trailing behind in sun hats and long mackintoshes, prepared for both sunshine and showers!

It was the first of many picnics, and I had only to collect them, and count them, occasionally. The children did the rest. Boys gathered firewood and made a fire, older girls did the cooking, little ones paddled in a shallow stream, and the scamps played Cowboys and Indians.

'You're crazy, sweetheart!' said Paul, tolerantly, when I told him about it; and increased my allowance!

For three years my precious manuscript travelled around to more than a dozen publishers, and three times my obliging typist made fresh copies at a reasonable cost. The reasons given for all these rejections were varied and amusing – 'The story falls into no particular category, for it is neither entirely secular, nor entirely theological' – 'It is not a story for children, but will probably meet the requirements of a Bible class' – 'It is too imaginative' – 'It is not imaginative enough' – 'There is no market for books of a religious nature' – and so on. But the majority had enclosed a small printed slip – 'We regret this script is not suited to our present requirements.' This was so coldly impersonal, I was chilled and upset, for I could imagine a young office boy, chewing gum, with one pile of rejection slips, and another pile of manuscripts. And every one of these scripts, no matter how trite and tawdry, would be the brainchild of its author. Its rejection had the same hurt as a rejected child to its mother.

But still I had mentioned it to nobody, for I was reluctant to admit I had failed again, in particular to my nearest and dearest. I was disappointed but not dismayed. One day I should hold a book in my hands with my name on its cover! One day, I would go into a bookshop and find a book of mine on the crowded shelves! But neither Paul, nor Mother, nor my sister Mary could understand dedication to an ambition still unrealized at the age of forty. They saw it as an unfruitful hobby, never likely to blossom into the reality of publication. I had long since stopped boasting of the best-selling novel I was going to write as soon as the war was over. But during the second Winter at the cottage, when the garden was sleeping again, and all creative outdoor work had finished till early

Spring, I began a second story book for children. Rejection had not cured me of stubbornness, for the second story also had a Biblical theme, but this time it was pure fantasy, and so ridiculous, I chuckled at the antics of the Noah family, and the animals they housed in the ark. Large and small, fierce and timid, clean and dirty, they kept their individual character throughout the long siege of the Great Flood. I was sorry for the zebras, with their weak stomachs, suffering from seasickness; for the lion with not enough space for his prowling; for the pigs with no muck to roll in, and the adventurous ram with his timid spouse. The giraffes were the first to see a speck of land on the horizon, the owls could not resist a tasty meal of mouse, or the monkeys refrain from squabbling and mischief. This second story had none of the seriousness of the first. Perhaps the children had inspired it during the hours we spent in the woods, or I saw with fresh eyes this favourite story of the infants school.

During the third Winter, I wrote *Mary Magdalene* – only to discover the story had recently been written and published by a well-known author!

I had collected my Sunday School prizes and the books I had received as presents in childhood, to bring back to the cottage as a small lending library for the Saturday Club in the Winter months. But only a few of the children had the time or inclination to read, and the comics entertained them for a brief half-an-hour every week. Only ten-year-old Bob, a studious boy who went on to Grammar School, and the two little sisters who had worn the sun hats and mackintoshes on our first picnic, went off happily with books, and returned them promptly in good condition.

Paul paid for the pantomime after Christmas, and I booked the front row of the gallery, and took them all by bus in a snow blizzard!

It seemed to me, during those three happy, contented years, that the Fates had been kind to us, and we would continue this way of life indefinitely. There were only the three short periods in the year to be separated from my beloved – to feel the heart sink, the tears hot, the voice crying after him – 'Goodbye, my darling. Come back soon!' And the anxious hours of waiting in the long Winter evenings. Was he drinking too much? Was he spending too much? I knew he had always been the first to buy a round of drinks at the hostel, the first to offer his cigarettes, for Bill had told me, and asked Paul, 'Who do you think you are then, Guv? – a bloody millionaire! One of these days you might need some of the cash you're chucking around!'

Suddenly, for no apparent reason, during the end of the third year, the children began to drift away. Some of the older children had left, and had been replaced by younger ones. Paul suggested they might be bored, and had found new interests, but that reason would not apply to all the children at the same time. I was puzzled and a little hurt that they simply stayed away, and sent no message.

Then, one Saturday morning, only Brenda arrived. She was twelve years old now, and a great favourite with me. She was still drawing, and I heard some time later she had won a scholarship to the College of Art. She was a quiet, well-behaved child, and she took her drawing book and pencil to the table now, and no longer sprawled on the floor.

But when I put down a glass of lemonade and her special kind of biscuit, she shook her head and burst into tears.

'Mummy told me not to stop, and I am not allowed to come any more. She said – she said Mr Taylor lives here, and you are not properly married.'

And she ran away, sobbing.

* * * * *

The end of the chapter at the American Base came as suddenly and dramatically as it began. Major Robert S. Martin was posted to the States, and his department was taken over by a younger man who made sweeping changes in administration. Paul's authority was negligible, Nellie and Ada put on their hats and coats for the last time. Complaints and criticism poured into Paul's office and he became tense and irritable. The new chief barked orders like a sergeant-major on a parade ground, and they trod on each other's toes at every step!

Meanwhile I hadn't quite recovered from that child's blurted truth. I avoided the village, stopped going to church, and took my long country walks in isolated lanes. Paul had been sympathetic, but surprised it had lasted so long. One spiteful tongue could soon infect the rest with suspicion and distrust. The Saturday Club for Children was finished for ever, and I put away the games and cards, tucked the books back in the shelves, and cancelled the weekly comics. The old pram had finally collapsed, but my two favourite urchins took away the wheels.

I wept too easily again. The mother's recent condemnation had revived all the old doubts and frustration. 'I wanted a home and a husband, and a child of my own. Was it asking too much? Why did it have to be you? Why?' I sobbed unreasonably one evening, after I had waited for hours, listening to the loud ticking of the clock, for Paul to come home.

Then he had taken my tear-wet face in his hands, and said, gently, 'But, my darling, you have a home and a husband, and you refused to have a child.'

'I know! I know! Don't remind me, and now it's too late!'

'What's wrong, sweetheart? What more can I do?'

'Nothing! Nothing!'

His tenderness bound me closer than passion, closer than anything he could say or do.

'You have only to tell me what it is you want, and I will get it for you.'

'I want nothing - only you.'

'But you have me.'

'For always?'

'For always,' he echoed.

That Saturday night, I opened the door to a flushed, grinning face, and a slurred voice announced importantly, 'Been chucked out! Sacked! Dishmished!'

'Paul Taylor, you're drunk!' I told him.

Stepping carefully over the threshold, he wagged a finger in my face. 'My darling sweetheart - Paul is never drunk - never! Jush a little intox - intoxicated,' he corrected haughtily. 'But I do apoloshize.'

'For what? - for getting drunk, or getting the sack?' I began to giggle, but he was deadly serious.

'For calling my super - superior officer a bastard!' He shook his head, trying to shake off the memory of what must have been an extremely angry finale.

'Oh, sit down, Paul, for heaven's sake, and stop rocking about on your toes. You make me dizzy.' I pushed him on to the sofa, but he jumped up, and gripped my shoulders.

'Lishen to me. You must lishen. It's vere, vere important,' he insisted. ' "Major," I said, "You can stick it up your jumper"

– then I walked right out and found another job – jew believe me?'

'I believe you,' I said, for he wouldn't lie to me. I pushed him back on the sofa, took off his shoes, and put on his slippers. 'So that's what you've been celebrating? You big baby. Aren't you ashamed of yourself?' Now I was torn between laughter and tears. What had he done? Where would he go?

'Kiss me!' he commanded. His breath stank of whisky, but I reached up my hands to clutch his head, as his mouth closed on mine. The firelight flicked on his broad brow, damp with sweat, and our two bodies trembled and melted together. He was my man, and I was his woman. This was our life – brief periods of peace and contentment till the pattern changed. There was no escape from the truth that we were pursued by our own shadows – the shadows of two people who could not make roots, could not retrace their steps, could not rectify their mistakes. I would go on a little more wary, not quite so trusting, but still I must go on, for those who dispense with the formalities of convention are fugitives of society.

'Did you say *Tuesday?* – this coming Tuesday?' I asked the following morning.

'Yes, Tuesday,' he murmured.

I sat up suddenly. 'But that's only two days!' I wailed.

He shivered as my warm body slid away. 'Don't get so het up, sweetie, Lie down again. There's bags of time.'

My head fell back on his shoulder.

'That's better. Now, what do you want to know?'

'Everything! Start at the beginning.'

'Okay,' he yawned expansively. 'Get me a cigarette, then I'll begin.'

Hiding the fact that he had been sacked from the Base – or sacked himself? – Paul had been to London, to interview the boss of a new holiday camp to be opened at Easter. On the strength of a glowing letter of recommendation from Major Martin, he was appointed Catering Manager.

A week later, he had visited the site – when I thought he was still busy at the Base. When I say Paul never lied to me, I mean, deliberately. This was a subtle form of deception, for my sake, to spare me a repetition of the anxiety I had known in 1946. It was easy to imagine the state of his mind, however, when strong emotions and pent-up anger had resulted in this final scene with Major X. Immediately he would be confronted by the question: 'What do I do now?' Two homes, two wives and a child depended on a regular income. He must have been a very worried man for the past month, and a very convincing applicant for the coveted post at the holiday camp. It would be mean to remind him of the fact it was only seasonal. Eight months at the most, then another job to be found before next Winter.

'Sufficient to the day,' I told myself, and settied down to listen.

'The place looks deserted, but that's to be expected in February. I guess it will soon take shape, once the skeleton staff take over next month. Basically, it's well planned, with rows of chalets, main offices, dance hall, bar, tuck-shop and snack bar, and a swimming pool. The grounds cover several acres, but I just glanced at it, for I was only interested in the kitchens and dining hall. The boss explained they would accommodate a thousand people, at two sittings, for meals.'

'It sounds just the job for you, darling,' I interrupted. 'But where do I come into it?'

'There would be a part-time job for you, in my office – simple book-keeping, checking invoices, answering the 'phone, and that sort of thing. I could put you on the canteen pay-roll from March first – as Mrs Taylor – and don't you forget it!'

'Where do we live?'

'In a comfortable chalet behind the main offices, and we can have our meals sent over from the kitchen,' he explained importantly.

'What are we doing about the cottage, Paul? We are coming back here, aren't we? You haven't any more surprises up your sleeve?' I asked suspiciously.

'Of course we are coming back. This is our home, and you can come back for a couple of days any time you like during the season, just to keep an eye on the place. I shan't get back, of course, till the end of October, for I must pop over to Ireland when the camp closes,' he reminded me.

'Yes, I suppose so,' I sighed. 'Well, tell me the rest. It sounds interesting. It will make a nice change – as Mother would say!'

He squeezed my shoulders affectionately, and asked, 'How come you're such a sweetie?' and went on – 'I shall need a whole month to get the place properly organized – order supplies, check on equipment, and engage staff. I've been given a free hand in my department, and there's a Manager in full charge of the camp – Bob Ingram – a nice guy. I've met him. As far as I'm concerned, my top priority is a good chef and pastry-cook, and one of my first jobs will be to interview the two who have been recommended by an old friend of mine in London. For the rest, my sweet, we take what comes, engage the pick of the bunch, and send the rest home. I wish I could take Doris and Ada along for the washing up!'

'Shall you like it?' I asked, doubtfully.

'Yes, providing they let me alone to run my department in my own way. It's a new challenge, sweetheart.'

'Yes, that's true.'

'We shall think we are back at the hostel, with everyone called by their Christian names.'

Then we were silent for a long moment, our separate thoughts travelling back to a time when we had few worries, once our attachment had been accepted.

'Let's not look back, my love, for it only makes us sad. We shall manage. And I shall quite enjoy a fresh bit of coastline with cliffs and caves,' I decided.

'Well, the scenery won't bother me. I shall be too busy to notice it. It's another of those places where everyone works flat out all the time. That suits me fine. I can't see myself sunbathing, or swimming in the pool!'

'Neither can I – you are just not the type!' I giggled.

It was bleak on that rocky coast in early March. The sea was grey, and a tearing wind blew across the deserted camp. We shivered as we stepped out of the taxi we had taken from the station. Paul dumped the bags on the forecourt, and clasped my hand. Seagulls swooped and screeched overhead. But we walked into the main lobby with bold resolution, smiling determinedly.

Bob Ingram hurried out of the office with outstretched hands.

'I'm sorry, Paul. I didn't hear you arrive or I would have been out there to welcome you.'

He gripped Paul's hand, and I was introduced.

'My wife, Sarah.'

We smiled politely at each other, but it was a mutual liking from that first moment.

'I've got the chef and the pastry-cook in my office now. Would you like to see them, Paul, or shall I ask them to wait?' he was saying.

'I will see them now,' Paul told him, and dropped my hand.

'Good show! Then I will leave you to it, and take your wife along to your chalet. I hope you won't mind everyone calling you by your Christian name, Mrs Taylor, but it is customary at a holiday camp.'

'Not at all,' I murmured, and we walked away together, while he called over his shoulder, 'George! Just bring those bags along, will you please.'

Yes, it was going to be all right!

Some two hours later, Paul joined me in the chalet. I had seen the housekeeper, collected blankets, linen and towels, unpacked, and had a cup of tea, with this pleasant-faced woman – one of several local women I could see busy with the chalets.

'Well, that's settled, thank God, but I had to 'phone the boss to sanction higher rates of pay. He was a bit dubious, but then he agreed it was a good policy. Then we all had a drink together in Bob's office, and now they are on their way back to London with a contract for the season,' Paul told me.

I could see his eyes flicker over the twin beds, with a dividing table, and he pushed them together against the wall.

'I knew you would do that,' I chuckled, as he pulled me into his arms.

'Why, you're frozen!' he frowned.

'It is a bit chilly after our cosy little cottage, but it's newly built.'

'I'll see Bob right away. We must have an electric fire, and a kettle, then you can make tea and coffee independently.'

And he went off with the air of a man who was accustomed to getting what he wanted, and came back with both articles, brand new from the stores!

Soon I had coffee brewing for Paul, and the strong aroma, in the chalet, so much like my room at the hostel, brought back more nostalgic memories.

'No cleaning here, remember!' Paul reminded me.

'You're the boss!'

On two separate hooks I had hung Paul's hat, and the small

wooden crucifix he had received at his First Communion.

'Now I know it will be okay when I see that,' said Paul, sentimentally.

Then he told me he had spoken to the boss about putting me on the pay roll, and £5 weekly had been agreed on for a six-hour day, plus board and lodging.

'Will that suit you, Mrs Taylor?' he asked, with a grin.

And I hugged him gratefully, for independence was still sweet, and without work I should be lost and miserable.

It was fascinating to see the camp taking shape all around us in that first month. Gay colour schemes of green and orange, flower beds, and tubs of tulips, stacks of deck chairs and striped awnings. Paul was busy all day and half the night, and I saw him only for hurried meals in our chalet, but he was happy again, and Bob liked him. He spent a lot of time interviewing staff. They came in all shapes and sizes – waitresses, kitchen porters, vegetable cooks, bartenders, cleaners, tuck-shop assistants, and washing-up women.

'Don't worry too much about it, old chap. Very few of the originals will stay all the season, and we can get any amount of students in the Summer Vacation,' Bob advised carelessly, for he already had several years' experience of holiday camps.

I would walk along the beach before breakfast, and it was good to come back to the chalet to see George staggering in with a tray, and to smell bacon and eggs. We all fed like fighting cocks, for Paul had engaged a local cook to look after us till the chef arrived.

'Well, my sweet, it's not exactly my idea of Paradise, but we have a bit of privacy, and we are together, not separated for seven or eight months,' he whispered, as we waited for our first campers that Saturday morning. He squeezed my hand, then he was swallowed up in the crowd.

We opened on a wild wet day in Easter week, and when the first coaches arrived, all the staff was there to welcome them – lined up with big smiles, like a regiment on the forecourt. A buffet lunch awaited them, with a promise of a turkey dinner in the evening, but the chilly travellers had to be comforted with hot soup. Bowls of salad were left untouched, and even the children shivered at the mention of icecream.

I was standing in the background, watching the scene, listening to the clamour of voices and cutlery, when Bob Ingram strode up to me.

'This blasted rain!' he grumbled. 'Let's hope it's a good omen for a fine Summer.'

He was disappointed, however, for it was one of those fitful Summers with more wet days than fine, and very windy.

'Bob, I should like to help with the smaller children if Katie needs another pair of hands. Paul doesn't need me in the office all day, and I haven't enough to do.'

'Good show!' he grinned, and hurried away.

But that first wet day was a foretaste of the effort and energy to be expounded on entertaining the campers indoors. The swimming pool, the green lawns, and the children's playground were deserted, while they grumbled and groused at the fickleness of the weather. Food and Entertainment were top priority, and appetites were enormous.

Danny, our Entertainments Manager, worked harder than anyone. 'Auntie Katie' was young, gay and attractive, and I helped her to round up the little ones to take them off to the big playroom. They followed her in a long train, and weary parents heaved sighs of relief as they shunted past. We followed the same pattern all the season, with Saturday the most exhausting day of the week for the staff. Satisfied campers departed, and new ones arrived, a little suspicious of all those big smiles on the forecourt!

I went back to the cottage for a couple of days once a month to weed the garden, and open the windows, but it was silent and empty without Paul. It was a pleasant enough way to spend eight months of the year, however, and we agreed to go back the following season. Bob Ingram would be there, also Danny and his wife, Katie, and Annie, the housekeeper. The boss was planning a big advertising campaign for the Winter, and offered Paul the job of 'Publicity Manager'. There would be a lot of travelling, but a generous salary plus expenses.

'I may have to be away from home quite a lot. Will you mind,' he asked me, anxiously, 'with no children and no gardening? How will you pass the time?'

'Scribbling,' I said, vaguely.

'Are you holding out on me? Are you writing that best-seller?'

'Not yet.' I changed the subject quickly.

It was late October when Paul carried our bags up the lane. He had been to Ireland for ten days, while I stayed at the camp, helping Annie to pack away blankets, and sort all the dirty linen for the laundry. It was good to be home again. We snatched off our hats and coats, and I put a match to the fire, while Paul sank into the folds of the old sofa. We looked at each other and smiled, complacently.

'Let me feel you,' he said, and his hands slid over my face, like a blind man groping for features he had forgotten.

'I've hardly seen you all Summer, he complained. Let's go to bed.' We were laughing as we went upstairs.

'This publicity stunt is way up my street, sweetheart. I can charge up all my expenses – first class you bet!' Paul told me, wickedly, and went off to a conference in early November, of which the boss's son, Richard, just down from Oxford, was an interested member. He promised to 'phone me every evening at seven o'clock, and kept his word no matter how pressing his engagements. The tone of his voice told me how much he was enjoying this job – meeting people, talking his head off, the best hotels and restaurants – he was back where he belonged, and there was no disguising the fact. Yet I was still determined to keep the cottage, and desperately afraid to give it up. I must have a home, and Paul a base.

'I can live any place, sweetie, but I must have you,' he had told me gaily, as he hurried back to that wider world that his gregarious appetite needed.

Then, after nearly two weeks away, he 'phoned me one evening from Brown's Hotel.

'Sweetheart, I can't get back for another week or so. I am absolutely up to my eyes in engagements. But you could come up here and join me for a couple of days. You can amuse yourself in the museums and art galleries during the day, and we can see a show or a film in the evening.'

I gasped in dismay, but he was not listening.

'You must come, my sweet, I need you,' he insisted.

'All right, darling, I'll come.'

It was Paul's trump card. Something in me had to respond to that pleading. 'I need you.' Something in me had responded to my 'boys' at the hostel.

'They need me, Paul,' I had told him.

'You're just a softie!' he jeered.

I sighed, but listened carefully to his instructions. I must take a taxi from the station to the hotel, where he would meet me in the lounge. If he was not there, I was to stay there, and not move, for he would be back like a shot after the afternoon engagement.

'Bless you! Till tomorrow.'

He hung up as I echoed, 'Till tomorrow.'

Paul had been trying to persuade me to buy some new clothes since the end of clothing coupons, but I had postponed a trip to Bath for I liked the feel of well-worn clothes, and had no need to dress up in the country. But now I saw myself arriving at Brown's Hotel in a shabby pre-war costume, and shoes that had been repaired a number of times. Paul still looked well-dressed and distinctive, in any one of three pre-war Savile Row suits, a pre-war overcoat, and the homburg hat, but my own clothes had been bought, as always, with the limited amount of money I could spare for dress. Might he be a little ashamed of me? I was not sure what his reactions would be in a superior West End hotel, but I knew that he was a different Paul away from me and the cottage, as I had realized when I saw him in the new environment of the holiday camp. Every time he departed for Ireland he was a different person, and I lost him even before he stepped on the train. The big, rather strutting stranger, with the brief-case, and the homburg hat, had an air of worldliness that left me alone and miserable on the platform. But the stranger that went away came back to me in his familiar guise, waving jauntily, calling 'Hi! Sweetheart!'

I knew which of these men I should be meeting in London, and it was not the one I liked best!

He strode briskly into the lounge, and came towards me, frowning, and his glancing kiss held no warmth. My head was throbbing, after my first permanent wave, and my feet squeezed uncomfortably into a pair of new shoes. The unaccustomed feel of new clothes – a navy blue costume and matching hat – did nothing for my morale. I was a stranger even to myself, and, apparently, a stranger to Paul. He took my arm, possessively, and led me away to Reception, to sign the register. And without a second's hesitation, I picked up the pen and wrote 'Sarah Shears'.

We went upstairs, his arm still tucked in mine, but for me it was the last straw, and I sat on the edge of the bed, wailing!

'Now I've ruined everything! I wish I hadn't come!'

'For God's sake, what's the matter with you?' he demanded. 'And what have you done to yourself? You look like a tart with all those damn curls and lipstick! And that hat, it's too big. You should always wear a small little hat.'

He snatched it off and tossed it on the dressing-table.

'Just look at your hair! You little fool! They've ruined it. You had pretty hair with a natural wave – and it stinks of lacquer!' he groaned, pressing his nose to the mop of stiff curls. 'So you have bought a new costume at last. Stand up and turn around.'

I obeyed, still sniffing miserably.

'You didn't give yourself enough time over choosing it. A size smaller would have been a better fit, but it's not bad. Why were you limping when we came upstairs?'

'My shoes – they pinch.'

He pushed me back on the bed, and pulled them off. Then he took a clean white handkerchief from his pocket, and rubbed my lips clean of lipstick. I was limp as a rag doll. My stomach was sick, and the back of my head throbbing with nerves. The symptoms were too familiar to be shrugged away – it was the beginning of a migraine attack, and nothing in this world would stop it at this stage. I began to cry again, weakly, and despairingly, and he stood there, undecided, for a long moment, then pulled me into his arms.

'Sweetheart – sweetheart – sweetheart. I don't *want* you any different. Stay the way you've always been, I like you that way. Okay?'

'Okay,' I whispered.

'And when you get back home, you just wash out all that stinking lotion and lacquer. I like it smelling of lemons. It was smelling of lemons that day I arrived at the hostel. I guess it was my fault for trying to mix business with pleasure. It never did work, not for me anyway.'

'I'm sorry, darling, about the register. Is it very embarrassing?'

'How many times do I have to repeat – you can't ever embarrass me. You are the only one to get embarrassed, my sweet innocent!'

But I could see he was still puzzled and annoyed that I could make such a stupid blunder.

'I'm sorry, darling,' I repeated, contritely. 'But I was so hot and bothered, I quite forgot I was Mrs Taylor.'

'Then I shall have to remind you, shan't I?' he threatened. 'Get undressed and into that bed!'

'Yes, darling,' I agreed, meekly.

'Not another migraine? My God! – and we were having dinner with the boss and his son, and Bob Ingram. They were all staying here.'

I shook my head and buried my face in the pillow. 'What a woman! What a wife!'

I could hear water splashing in the basin, and the hairbrush clatter on the dressing table.

'So long, my sweet. Try to sleep,' he said carelessly, and the door closed. It was, for both of us, a great mistake to mix business with pleasure!

The second season at the holiday camp was merely a repetition of the first. Then, in October, the boss announced that his son, Richard, would be taking over all the catering the following year.

'He's been picking my brains for weeks, that young upstart!' Paul exploded wrathfully.

It was true. He had.

* * * * *

When the parcel was delivered to the cottage one morning in November, I held it for a long moment with my arms wrapped around it, like a mother embracing a lost child.

'My book – it's my book,' I whispered.

'Well, come on, open it up!' Paul insisted.

We were badly in need of some kind of boost to our morale, for it was the end of another chapter, and Paul, once again, faced unemployment.

'I c-can't b-believe it,' I stammered.

'Well, come on! Open it up! Let's have a look at this masterpiece!'

He handed me a penknife to cut the string, and we stood there, on either side of the table, with the parcel between us, and I was so nervous Paul had to cut the string and take off the wrapping. The six presentation copies which every author receives on publication held the clean, distinctive smell of fresh print, and the cover picture was a reproduction of a Biblical painting.

Paul was silent.

'Aren't you pleased?' I asked, tentatively.

'I'm afraid,' he said.

'Afraid? But why, my darling?'

'It's the beginning for you, the end for me.'

'No! Don't say that! It's not true!' I pushed the books away, and flung my arms around his neck. 'Now listen to me, for a change, will you, *please!* This is not going to make the slightest difference to *us.* You needn't worry. I shall never write a best-seller. This is only a small drop in the ocean of books published every year. Five hundred copies may be sold, perhaps, then finished, forgotten. My second manuscript is going round the publishers the same way, but again, only a limited number of people will buy it, even if I get it accepted. This publisher was not interested in a second Biblical story, so I had to start all over again to find another. The third story won't even see the light of day. Would you believe it, *Mary Magdalene* has already been written and published in a new version only last year!' I laughed at myself, to prove my own stupidity, but Paul shook his head.

'One day, you will be a successful author,' he said.

'Never! Not at my age!' I told him, passionately. 'And if you are going to get upset, I shall not send out any more stories. I shall write them, because I can't help myself, and I have to write, but they needn't be published.'

Now I had to speak quickly and urgently, to get it all over at once, what I had to say, for this would hurt him, and he could be very angry.

'Darling, I've sold the copyright and paid the rent for another year. You don't mind, do you? Say you don't mind. I love it here. It's selfish of me, but if we could stay a bit longer – just another year, perhaps? Then I will go away with you – anywhere, I promise!'

'You sold the copyright to pay the rent?' he repeated.

I nodded, and burst out again, in a fever of anxiety, 'Darling, *please* let me help. Just the rent and the fuel until you are back in circulation again. To tell you the truth, I have ordered another ton of logs, and half a ton of coal,' I confessed.

Paul pushed me away, and flicked over a page of the top book in the pile. Then he stopped, and read aloud, 'I dedicate this book in affection and admiration to Paul Taylor.'

Now he was choked with emotion, and he could only look at me, smiling, astonished.

'I wanted to say, "I dedicate this book to my adored husband", but that would be dishonest, wouldn't it?'

He nodded, his eyes moist. And we looked at each other in complete agreement now, and both were satisfied. Then he turned the pages reverently, and went back to the title page to read the dedication again. His face was eager, glowing with pride and satisfaction.

'My darling sweetheart – this calls for a celebration. Dinner in town! Champagne! – the lot!'

'I should love a cup of tea, and a slice of hot buttered toast. Would you get that for me? It would suit me so much better than dinner in town, with champagne.'

He yelled with laughter, and snatched me into his arms. 'I shall wait on you like a queen, my sweet,' he promised.

And I curled myself up on the sofa, waiting for the tea and toast – feasting my eyes on the six new books.

* * * * *

'I entertained an editor to-day!' I told Paul, excitedly, when he returned from an interview at Bristol, three months later. 'He came to tell me I was one of ten finalists in a short story contest, but not, unfortunately, in the first three to win a prize. Imagine coming all the way from London to tell me that! He has asked me to write more stories for his weekly periodical for women – homely, unsophisticated stories. He 'phoned to ask if it would be convenient to call on me, and gave no reason, so I could only suppose it was somebody checking on you, darling, since you had to cut Jacqueline's allowance after Christmas. You know – a private detective. Was I relieved when he told me he was an editor!'

'Your vivid imagination!' Paul jeered.

I sighed happily, as I pushed his feet into warm slippers, and went on, 'I gave him a mushroom omelette for lunch, and some of your Camembert cheese. Then we just sat here beside the fire, and talked for a couple of hours or more. Naturally I did most of the talking.'

'That's a change if nothing else.' His voice was flat, and he reached for a cigarette.

'What's the matter? Have you had a tiresome day? Did you not get the job?'

'Yes, I got it, but it's a lousy job. I can't see myself as a warden at a hostel for overseas students,' he sighed heavily.

'Poor darling. Do you want me to come and live in Bristol, or can you get home once a week?'

'One free day and night. I have a deputy to leave in charge. No, you stay here.'

'You're tired. I'll make fresh coffee, and I kept half the mushrooms for your omelette.'

I dropped a kiss on his bleak face and went to the kitchen – wishing I had kept my news till later, but it was not often I had such an unexpected and welcome visitor, and my first impulse was to share it with Paul. My thoughts were still on the stories I would write, and when a horrid smell of burning drifted into the sitting-room, Paul leaped to his feet, and hurried into the kitchen.

'Well, if that's a sample of the omelette you served to your editor, he is not likely to be back! Get out of my way, woman. 'I'll make my own omelette. Call yourself a cook!' he jeered, as he beat fresh eggs in a basin.

Now the dreary day in Bristol was forgotten. The omelette was perfect, and he finished the Camembert cheese.

This Bristol job lasted exactly six months, then a married couple was engaged as houseparents, and Paul came home.

We sat down together one evening on the old sofa, to talk it over sensibly. It was Paul's suggestion, and it seemed the answer to our immediate problem. I was still hanging on, stubbornly, to Willow Cottage, while Paul was straining to get away. He saw it now as a prison without bars, not a haven of contentment. But for me it was still a sanctuary, and I was earning a little money – enough to cover my personal expenses for travelling to Worthing to visit Mother, and to pay a typist to prepare the scripts.

'If we get the owner's sanction to sub-let the cottage for six months, we could take separate jobs, save on rent, fuel and housekeeping, and try to get our affairs straightened out,' Paul suggested.

I knew this was not the only reason that he wanted to get away for a time. My small success with the writing was a constant reminder of his own failure.

So I ordered a copy of *The Lady* to be sent to me every week, and scanned its pages carefully, while Paul scanned the lists of vacancies from an agency.

'What exactly are you looking for?' he asked me one Thursday morning.

'Anything! – listen to this – "Mother's help wanted. Fond of children and animals. Country situation. Buckingham. Good wages. Box number," – or this – "Housekeeper to retired Company Director. Top salary. Lovely home. Box number." '

'It could be the answer, my sweet. He would probably have a heart attack and die on the golf course, and leave you all his money. You would have to sleep with him, of course!' he reminded me, carelessly.

'Wouldn't you be jealous?'

'Like hell I should! You could think of me in the queue at the Labour Exchange.' His voice was so bitter my eyes swam with tears.

'It's all my fault. I've got you into this mess. If I hadn't begged you – if. . .'

'Stop it!' he shouted, harshly. 'You know darn well it's not your fault. Don't talk such crazy rot!'

'Then don't shout at me!'

A slow grin spread over his face. 'My, my, my fierce little sweetheart! You should do it more often, I reckon. I do apologize.'

And we went on, scanning the 'Situations Vacant'. I had already decided the country post would suit me, and an interview was arranged the following week. Since the family in Buckinghamshire were moving to Scotland in April, a six months' engagement was agreed on.

'It's so much easier for a woman to get a job since the war,' I told Paul, for he was naturally a little envious of my easy success. But time was running out, and the sub-tenants moving in on the first day of October. When he told me he was taking a job as a waiter at a Bournemouth hotel, I was shocked and dismayed, but he shrugged indifferently.

'What do I care? It's a job, and it can't be worse than this God-forsaken place,' he added, thoughtlessly, and tried, too late, to make amends.

'So that's how you see it now – God-forsaken?' It saddened me, for now I knew for certain I should have to leave my dream cottage next year.

So I went off to Buckinghamshire, and Paul to Bournemouth. It was the longest six months I had ever known, and I wrote to him every day, and posted the epistle twice a week. Paul had no time or inclination to write letters, so he sent telegrams instead – it did not occur to him that a telegram cost so much more than a letter. They were so tenderly worded, I would cry over them in the privacy of my bedroom.

'Thank you sweetheart for your marvellous letters. Thinking of you keep smiling all my love Paul.' was typical of a number of telegrams I received during that interminable Winter. But I still can feel the warmth of that wonderful reunion, and hear my sobbing voice on the station platform. 'Never again! – Never, never again!'

'Never again, sweetheart!' Paul echoed, as his strong arms enfolded me. 'Kiss me!' he demanded.

'Take it easy now, Guv. Them sort of kisses is highly dangerous!' said the cheeky porter. Then, remembering his duty – 'Carry your bags, sir? Taxi, sir?'

* * * * *

It was time for another visit to Ireland. Paul had been over for a few days before he went to Bournemouth, and now he must go again. What did he actually tell them about his circumstances? I wondered. Would that child he adored ever know the truth about us, and about her father's slow climb down the ladder of prosperity? Jacqueline had been so annoyed about the cut in her allowance, I would not have been surprised to see her at the door. She wrote – 'I must remind you, Paul, that whatever your circumstances in Somerset, you are still under an obligation to your legal wife. The money I earn independently, as a hair-dresser, is my own, and has nothing to do with the allowance. Rosalinde will be leaving the Convent next year, and there will be fees to pay at the School of Drama in Belfast. She has set her heart on the stage, so it is no use trying to dissuade her. If she is as good an actress as her father an actor, we should see her on the West End stage some day!'

This was a sample of Jacqueline's wry humour, and yet another reminder of her 'rights' as a wife and mother. She, too, held a trump card – the girl – for whatever she wanted she must have, and Paul could deny her nothing – dancing lessons, music, horse-riding, and now the Drama School. He would keep the image of a proud and generous father until she was married. But it seemed he had long cherished a dream to get her to England when she had finished her formal education, and now he was disappointed.

'How come my dreams just break like pie-crust?' he had asked me, sadly, one day.

'What was the dream, my darling?'

'To have a flat in London, and Rosalinde living with us. I could see her with her own bed-sitting room, and her own friends coming in, and my daughter grown into an independent young woman, earning a good salary in dress designing, for she has a flair for it, and her mother has encouraged it. She has been making her own clothes, apart from school uniforms, for the past two years. This crazy idea of being an actress may be just another of the growing up stages. She's such a talented kid, she can do anything she sets her heart on,' he sighed.

But I passed no comment. I could not remind him that he once had promised me we should never have to meet – this child who shared his heart. And I could not tell him that I was still a little jealous of this child, and the years had not lessened the pangs of enforced separation three times a year. She was their daughter – Paul's and Jacqueline's – not mine. She would also drain him dry with her demands, unwittingly, for she would not know when he was poor, unemployed, and disillusioned. I would be the only one to know the truth about Paul Taylor. 'Too old at forty!' was the sad aftermath of war – and Paul was a man past fifty when he had that first interview, and came back to me so furiously angry and resentful. Now his anger and resentment had died, and he was moody and apathetic, jeering at my persistent optimism.

'Well, Mrs Micawber, when is your something going to turn up?'

I did not talk to him any more of my writing, or mention another small success – the publication of an illustrated booklet, to sell at half-a-crown. This was the popular story of a famous seafaring cat – and I kept the copyright.

Sometimes I found myself thinking about the man I had loved before the war on my first voyage to India. Would my life with him, if he had loved me, have been secure and successful? Perhaps, if I never went away, or had any chance of comparison, these small shadows of doubt would never intrude. But going to Worthing, to visit Mother, always unsettled me. I saw my younger brother, Henry, with a home, a wife, and a small son – a handsome, intelligent little boy, with lively dark eyes – my second nephew. Mother's probing questions and my own guilty blushes, had eventually disclosed the secret I had kept for so long.

'There is a man in that cottage of yours.'

It was a statement that could not be denied, I was still, fundamentally, her child, and all Mother's children were honest.

'Yes,' I had whispered.

'Married?'

'Yes.'

That was all, but here eyes were black, and her cool, precise voice condemned me as a fallen woman.

'Aren't you ashamed of yourself, Sarah?' she asked, scornfully.

And I went away in sorrow. She never forgave me. It was, for my steadfast, loyal Mother, the ultimate sin to separate husband and wife. 'Those whom God hath joined together let no man put asunder,' she would quote.

When we were little, and dependent on her for everything, she taught us we had to choose, one or the other – right or wrong – good or bad – true or false. Her principles were inflexible, and they had not weakened. I was still her child, but now she regarded me with a scornful pity – and asked no more questions. Even the autographed copies of my books, and the stories she read in the several periodicals to which I contributed, could not alter her opinion of me. I was, and always would be, the black sheep of her little flock. There was no softness in Mother. Her life had been hard, and she was hard – indestructible, but hard.

Paul came home from the 'Adam and Eve' for the last time. 'George and Mabel seemed quite upset to-night. "We shall miss you, luv," Mabel told me. "You've been the life and soul of the place for so long. Nobody to make us laugh with all their naughty stories!" '

'Of course they will miss you, darling,' I agreed placidly. Why remind him of something of which he was unaware - that while he sat silent and moody in his own home, he could still go out and amuse the customers of the little pub.

'Well, I reckon that will be the last drink for me in a country pub,' he said, but there was no regret in his voice, and there would be no nostalgia.

'The last time' - I shivered at the finality of those words. For the last time, I had made a bonfire and weeded the flower beds. For the last time, I had climbed over the stile and walked along country lanes where budding hedges, primroses and celandines reminded me it was Spring again. As though I had to be reminded! Spring was here, in my own garden, in the patch of purple and gold under the apple tree; the red squirrel, with his inquisitive eyes; the smell of damp earth; the song of the blackbird. But my heart had never known such anguish as it now knew. Tomorrow we must go from here, and now I was afraid - afraid of the future. Paul must never know that fear had driven out faith and hope and optimism. Mrs Micawber had fled, and taken Ruth with her, leaving me alone.

The two boxes were packed - one with blankets and linen, the other with crockery, pots and pans. Our three suitcases, the gramophone and my manuscripts, completed the packing. It seemed a very insignificant pile of luggage for two people, but it was all we possessed - apart from books which I had to leave behind, for there would be no space for books in the furnished rooms we were renting in Soho until we could find a flat.

Now the last busy week was over, the cottage clean, the garden tidy. I leaned on the window-sill for the last time, breathing in the fresh, cold air from the silent fields. The sky was studded with stars. A sense of utter desolation swept over me, and I covered my face with my hands and sobbed. Paul lifted me, and tucked me tenderly under the bedclothes; then he climbed in beside me, and cradled me in his arms. He knew, instinctively, it was not a lover I needed on this last night in the big bed with the brass knobs.

3

Lodging Places

'You must eat something, sweetheart. You had nothing yesterday. Try a little chicken?' Paul coaxed gently, as the train sped towards London. I shook my head.

'Another cup of tea?'

'Yes, please.'

'Waiter! – a pot of tea for my wife, and I'll take the steak and chips,' I heard him say.

'Sorry, sir, we don't serve tea with lunch, only coffee.'

'Now come *on*. Be a good guy. Supposing your wife was sick and couldn't take anything but tea?' The bantering charm did not deceive me, and I knew he could explode in a split second if he didn't get what he wanted.

'Okay?' he prompted, as the waiter still hovered uncertainly.

'Okay – when I've finished serving the soup.' He gave me a withering glance, but I was too miserable to care.

Paul covered up my silent misery with excited talk about his wonderful new prospects, but only half my mind attended to him to-day. I saw myself as an infant again, curled in the warmth of Mother's arms – detached, newborn, vulnerable.

Paul poured the tea. It was hot and sweet. Then he tipped the waiter generously, with his bright smile.

'A pleasure, sir. I hope the lady soon feels better.'

We left the rocking dining car, and went back to the empty carriage.

'First class?' I had murmured – thinking of the expense. But I was grateful for the unexpected luxury, and stretched out on the seat with my head in Paul's lap. He had taken off my shoes.

'Relax, sweetheart,' he said, soothingly – as gentle as a woman with a sick child.

I closed my eyes and slept for a while. When I awoke, I was startled and surprised to find myself on a train with Paul, for we always parted at the station, and had never travelled together. I sat up quickly to look at him. His face was so calm and composed we could have been taking a holiday together. Then I remembered, and shivered involuntarily. He drew me close, and kissed my cheek with cool lips.

'It's going to be all right, my sweet.' Paul was the comforter to-day, but then he was also the victor, and I the vanquished. He was doing what he wanted, at last. We were on our way to London, and we were not going back to Somerset, or the cottage, ever. Even with his comforting arm about my shoulders, the future seemed bleak, and I watched the quiet countryside slipping away through a mist of silent tears. Who would be picking my daffodils and tulips? Who would cut my little patch of grass? All my garden tools were left behind in the shed, together with the deck chairs.

Remembering – remembering – such awful desolation in remembering that patch of purple and gold under the apple tree. The end of another chapter – what next? But I was not yet ready to start, and we were rushing too quickly towards London.

'Talk to me, Paul,' I begged. I had to hear his confident voice again, to convince me he was right, and we hadn't made another dreadful mistake. Although he was so gentle with me to-day, I knew he was glad, and the old eagerness was stirring in his veins. There was no sensuality in his tender glances, or his cool lips, and his searching eyes saw beyond this peaceful landscape to the city we were fast approaching. All the apathy and depression was left behind in that empty cottage. Now he was alert and active again, straining towards a new way of life. With one hand he could take out a cigarette, and flick the lighter with easy nonchalance, while keeping the other pressed to my shoulder.

'Tell me again about this trade expedition, Paul. I was not properly listening the other night,' I confessed.

'I knew you weren't,' he smiled, indulgently, and began to tell me about a scheme that seemed too ridiculous to be taken seriously. 'But I've got a six months' contract, and anything can happen in six months, once I am back in circulation,' he had told me excitedly, when he came back from the interview.

And this time there was no pleading with him to stay, for my sake. The chapter was already closed when he hugged me exuberantly.

'A thousand a year, my sweet, and all my expenses!' He brought back a bottle of wine in his brief case that night, and we drank a toast to the brave new enterprise, – 'Trade Expeditions!'

I choked on the wine.

'What a baby you are! Drink up!' he teased me. 'It will get you into the right mood for making love!' He was irresistibly gay and charming that night. But he drank all the wine, for to my uncivilized palate it tasted as sour as vinegar!

It was an old man's brain-child, and he had spent several years of his retirement working on the idea, and persuading a number of his former colleagues in the City to invest some money in it. I saw it as a twentieth-century Marco Polo expedition, with mechanized vehicles instead of horses!

Paul had met the creator of this extraordinary gamble at the Piccadilly Hotel, and had laughed in his face when the maps were unfolded, and the scheme explained.

'It's crazy!' Paul told him. 'It's too fantastic to work – on paper, yes, but not in practice.'

But when he left the hotel, some three hours later, he was almost convinced, and had been appointed its first (and last) Publicity Manager.

'It will be my job to convince all those other dubious guys to invest their money in it, and I shall have a team of experienced salesmen to help me at this initial stage. We have to sell the project to at least five hundred manufacturers to make the scheme profitable. Can you imagine a two-mile caravan of trailers, travelling through Europe into Asia, exhibiting British made goods – anything from a wristwatch to a farm tractor?' he asked me, that night.

'I can, but I can't see any customers buying the goods.'

'They won't actually buy the goods on display, but place orders – a travelling Earl's Court is a better description.'

'Sounds like a travelling circus!' I teased him. 'I hope you are not thinking of going along?'

'Well, I wouldn't mind it if I could take my sweetheart!' His eyes twinkled with amusement at the thought, then he asked, 'Who am I to say it won't work? These guys are willing to pay me to sell space. I reckon I could sell them the English Channel!' and he yelled with laughter.

'But five hundred manufacturers? Where will you find them? The man's mad!' I told him, sipping the wine cautiously.

That had been a month ago, and now, when he repeated the story, and enlarged on its possibilities, it seemed even more improbable, and my heart sank. We had always enjoyed a challenge, but perhaps, for me, it had to be more substantial. This was so intangible, like a mirage in the desert – an old man's dream, not a reality.

But Paul was more far-seeing on this occasion. He would meet a lot of people, make useful contacts, then, if the project collapsed in six months, there could be another job waiting. It was not like me to stand, trembling, on the verge of a new chapter, reluctant to venture, fearful of the future.

'Tell me about these rooms in Soho. That's more important for me, at the moment, where we are going to live,' I told him briskly.

Then our eyes met, and smiled.

'That's better. That's my sweetheart.' His lips brushed mine. 'There's not much to tell, for I haven't actually seen the place. It was recommended by a guy I met in the bar, and I 'phoned to book the rooms before I left London. But it's only temporary, my sweet, and you can amuse yourself while I am in the office, tripping around London, looking for a flat. That's your baby. I shall leave it to you entirely. A month at the most in those rooms at Marie-Louise's place, then a place of our own again!'

'Marie-Louise? She's French?'

'Yes, didn't I tell you? What does it matter? We don't have to live with her. We have a separate sitting-room and bedroom, but you might have to share her kitchen, I forgot to ask.'

We were steaming into the London terminus, and there was no time to ponder over this disturbing fact. If we had only a sitting-room and bedroom, then obviously I should have to do our cooking in our landlady's kitchen.

Paul was out of the carriage and had grabbed a porter before I had put on my hat. Our boxes and cases were collected from the luggage van, and piled in the front of a taxi.

We climbed in, and Paul smiled, pleased with the speed of the operation. Then he took my hand in a strong, warm clasp. I was like a child, dependent on him for everything, and he took charge of me and our affairs as though he had never asked my opinion on anything. The traffic swirled around us, and the pavements were crowded with hurrying figures. I sat on the edge of the seat, clutching Paul's hand, praying for a miracle. If the taxi would change course, and return to the station from which we came, I should read 'Bath' on the notice board, and step into a westbound train. This sad day would be just a bad dream, and to-morrow morning I should wake up in the cottage again.

But there was no miracle, and we drove on towards Soho.

On the third floor of a house in a narrow street, Marie-Louise hung over the banisters, calling encouragement in a rough mixture of French and broken English.

'It's not my job,' grumbled the taxi-driver, panting under the weight of the linen-box. But since he had already accepted a generous tip to help us with the baggage, he could be as churlish as he pleased, while still obliging us.

We climbed the bare stairs slowly, and I headed the procession, with the gramophone and a bag of oddments I had pushed in at the last moment, when the cases were locked. Marie-Louise patted my hand absent-mindedly, but her eyes followed Paul, climbing the stairs with two heavy cases. He dropped them at her feet on the tiny landing, and swore at her in French. She retaliated with a squeal of shrill laughter, and they measured each other like a dog and a cat sparring for a fight. She was short and plump, with dyed hair piled in a tight coil on top of her head, and she was dressed in black, with a lot of jewellery, and stank of scent.

Paul placed an arm protectively about my shoulders. 'Madame, this is my wife.' We shook hands politely, and her eyes darted over my tweed coat and sensible country shoes.

'My wife is tired, Madame. We have had a long journey. She would appreciate a cup of tea,' Paul reminded her.

She spread her hands and shrugged. 'But certainly, Monsieur. But first, I show you my flat.'

Proudly she escorted us round her tiny penthouse apartment. It was exactly like a doll's house, and Paul looked huge as he followed her. There were four rooms, and we should have two. Marie-Louise was obviously very house-proud, for everything was clean and shining, but her kitchen was her main concern.

'The gas stove, she is beautiful, yes? I 'ave already eight years my stove. When you cook, you wipe 'er down,' she reminded me.

'Yes, Madame,' I answered obediently.

The kitchen table was fitted precariously over a high, old-fashioned bath.

'That's an awkward arrangement, Madame. Supposing we want to eat our dinner when you want to take a bath?' Paul teased her.

She gave him a saucy look, and answered in her mother tongue. When she had shown us the two tiny rooms we had been allocated, she went back to the kitchen to put on the kettle. 'What did she say to you, Paul?' I wanted to know.

He pulled me into his arms and translated. 'You are welcome, Monsieur, to see as much of me as you please!'

'What a cheek!'

'Leave her to me, sweetheart. I'll manage her,' he promised. 'Well, I guess it's been a bit of a shock. I do apologize. I should have checked on it. But I'll get you out of here as soon as I possibly can. If I pay her a month's advance rent to-day, we are free to leave whenever we like. Shall we manage, or shall we book into an hotel?'

'We shall manage. We can't afford hotels,' I told him decidedly. 'Unlock that case of yours, will you, darling. I put a clean tablecloth just inside, and there's a cake in the oddments bag. Why not ask Marie-Louise to make a pot of coffee as well as a pot of tea?'

He kissed me gratefully, and went back to the kitchen. The walls were so thin, I could hear their voices raised in argument. Paul had switched on the electric fire, for our rooms felt damp and chilly.

'She was demanding another pound a week for electricity, on top of the rent. There is no meter,' he explained, when he came back with the tea and coffee. 'In that case, my sweet, we will switch on that second bar!' he laughed, and added – 'She's just a trollop, and her language is foul!'

We spent six months with Marie-Louise, for the simple reason

I could find no other accommodation at a reasonable rent. Every week Paul opened his wallet and handed me a handful of notes, without even counting them.

'Do what you like with it, sweetheart. Spend it, save it, or find us a decent apartment,' he said, carelessly, that first week. I hurried to the Post Office to put it safely away in my bank book!

But the rents were exorbitant, or seemed so to me after paying only £8 a month for the cottage. Several house agents took our name and address, charged a fee and found us nothing but luxury flats. Newsagents advertised comfortable furnished rooms that, on inspection, were dreary and desolate basements, or stifling attics. I travelled on buses and walked miles, because I was too scared of the Underground escalators after so long in the country.

For Paul, the six months we spent in that crowded little penthouse was a joke, for he rather enjoyed the rough exchanges with Marie-Louise, and he was out all day, busy in his smart new office at Holborn, organizing the Trade Expedition.

But I was nervous of that sharp tongue and quick temper, and the migraine attacks were frequent and severe. Lying in bed, under the sloping roof, I would shed weak tears of self-pity, and long to be back at the cottage. But Paul was back in his natural element, and we couldn't both be happy and satisfied. I had had my way for seven years, and now it was his turn. His self-esteem was restored, and the old energy and enthusiasm was good to see.

'Sweetie, put on your hat, we can get our supper at "Rinaldi's". I can see by your face you've been in trouble with Marie-Louise again,' he told me one evening during our second week.

I nodded mutely, and he folded his arms around me.

'How come you can't stand up to her? It's not like you to be so meek.'

'I don't know. She makes me nervous. Even when she is out I am listening all the time for her to come back. And it's never a convenient time to use her kitchen. "Come back later," she tells me. It's hopeless!' I wailed.

'Poor sweetheart! I shall have to swear at her again. It's the only language she understands. But she must tell you a definite time to use her kitchen, and stick by it. We are paying her well. She must co-operate.'

But Marie-Louise just spread her hands and asked crossly, 'Why is she always washing her clothes? Every week she must wash! She must cook! She must wash! Is it 'er kitchen or mine? I do what I please in my own 'ouse, Monsieur!'

She had soon discovered we were not married. Tapping on our bedroom door early one morning, she waited for Paul to slip on his dressing-gown and turn the key in the lock, then she handed him a letter.

'For Miss Sarah Shears – your wife, Monsieur?' she asked, innocently.

'She is. Thank you, Madame.' Paul closed the door on her mocking laugh. It was a letter from Mother.

It became a habit (and a very pleasant habit for me, who had to bear with our landlady's erratic temperament) to walk round to 'Rinaldi's' for supper several times a week. Paul took me in turn to the other crowded restaurants in Soho – Spanish, Hungarian and French – but I liked the cosy atmosphere of Rinaldi's place. There were three generations in this Italian family, and the grandparents, aged about sixty, were still, very obviously, the proprietors of the restaurant. Sons were in the kitchen, sons' wives waiting at table, and two lively, black-eyed children had their own little table, upstairs, and sat there, quite unperturbed, eating mounds of spaghetti, on which grandpapa poured richly flavoured meat and gravy. Paul always greeted the proprietors in their mother tongue, and their worn, sallow faces lit with pleasure. Papa Rinaldi would take Paul's hand and fold it affectionately in his dry palms, then do the same for me, saying, in careful English, 'Good evening, Mrs Taylor. It is a pleasure to see you.'

Rinaldi had come to Soho as a young man, to work as a waiter and learn English. Then he went home to Italy, married his sweetheart, and came back to Soho to open their small restaurant. They prospered during the wars, with so many servicemen and women on leave in London, and now they were established, respected and popular. Only favoured customers could walk in and find a vacant table. Others had to book in advance.

Soho was a fascinating place, and its narrow crowded streets and cosmopolitan atmosphere appealed to me strongly. I avoided Mayfair, Bond Street, and the shopping centres of Regent Street and Oxford Street, but wandered around Soho, poking inquisitively into the delicatessen shops, where unidentifiable objects floated in tubs of vinegar! The Belgian pastry-cook had a tempting display of fresh pastries in the shop window every day, and crisp French loaves, hot from the oven. Paul would often come back with half-a-dozen pastries in a little box. We would eat them all during the evening with our tea and coffee, and not bother with supper.

But I missed the comfort and liveliness of our crackling wood fires and blazing coals. It was a damp, chilly Summer, I seem to remember, and the streets more often wet than dry. The electric fire soon made the room stifling hot, but Paul liked it stuffy. The room was so small it could only accommodate one armchair, so we shared it! Here we sat together in the late evening, exchanging news and views on the day's events.

Now that Paul had responsibility again, he was happy and confident, but also able to relax. It was natural to hear his boasting, to see his proud arrogance. This, too, was the man I had to love and admire. Back once more on the top of the ladder, he looked about him with bold, challenging glances. Nothing was impossible. No scheme was too improbable.

'One hundred-per-cent enthusiasm and efficiency – not ninety-nine-and-three-quarters!' he told his team of picked men. He could not stand half-hearted and desultory methods, or suffer fools gladly.

During the first week in London he had already selected five intelligent, experienced sales representatives – made redundant from their own firms through no fault of their own. The sixth man he chose for no other reason than he liked him – an ex-commando, with a limp and an irresistible grin. They met every day at Paul's office for a week, to discuss the routes they would follow by car and train. Their separate territories would cover the British Isles in the six months they had been allowed to persuade manufacturers to display their goods on the trailer caravan. Each man had a guaranteed £20 weekly, plus expenses. They all knew in their hearts Space was going to be a most difficult thing to sell.

'It's like selling blinkin' fresh air!' said the ex-commando, with a chuckle.

But, like Paul, they would sell themselves, and their personalities, to have a job, even for six months, for all were family men. They returned to London to report, receive their wages and expenses, every Friday night. They met in the lounge of a West End hotel, enjoyed a smoke and a drink together. I would accompany Paul, to sit and listen, for an hour or more, with a pot of tea at my elbow!

I could see that Paul's enthusiasm was infectious, and this team of men, so widely different in character and temperament, were giving of their best to an extraordinary gamble, doomed from the start. A lot of money had already been spent on blue-prints, brochures, advertising in the press, postage, telephone calls and two typists. They seemed to me like a group of little boys, eagerly exploring a new playground. For all their earnestness and energy, it was pathetically obvious to me, an onlooker, that it could not last beyond the six months, and would collapse as easily as a pack of cards. My heart wept for them - all seven - for I could feel their anxiety, their tense determination to sell a commodity that existed only on a blue-print.

Every week I banked as much money as could be spared from my careful housekeeping. Paul paid the rent and electricity, and argued with Marie-Louise over everything. She was mean and grasping. If she thought I was using too much gas, she would lock the kitchen and go out for the day, leaving me to weep angry tears of frustration. It was, for me, a very bitter experience, but also an awakening to further maturity.

'What does she do with herself all the time?' I once asked Paul. We were already in bed, and could hear a man's voice in the next room.

'My sweet innocent, she earns a living in the only way possible for a dame like Marie-Louise. It's the oldest profession in the world. That first statement of hers about the bath-tub put me wise to it. She was mad at me that I didn't catch on. She's still mad at me. I guess that's why she is always asking for more money for one thing and another. Well, I may as well tell you the rest, my sweet, since we've got on to the topic of Marie-Louise. On one of those evenings when you were in bed with a migraine, I went to the kitchen to make my own coffee, and found her sitting, stark naked, on a stool, drying her feet after taking a bath. "Come in, Monsieur," she invited me. And I stood in the doorway, in a sort of calm detachment, and told her, "Marie-Louise, you're a bitch!" Then I went round to "Rinaldi's" for the coffee, and stayed to supper.'

I shivered as his arms enfolded me lovingly, protectively. 'Paul – you wouldn't – ?'

He laughed softly. 'No, my sweet. I am much too fastidious. Besides, you've spoiled me for other women. I don't even see them. You do believe me?'

'Yes, I believe you.' And before he found my lips in the darkness, he whispered, 'It's only you, sweetheart, now and for ever.'

I remember the first time I managed to outwit Marie-Louise, and greeted Paul excitedly on the landing one evening – our tempestuous landlady was not yet back.

'Darling, I've done quite a big wash to-day! She went out after breakfast, and I dashed for the kitchen. When she came back I was hanging it out on the fire escape. She swore at me in French, but I was so pleased to get it done, for once I didn't mind her.'

'The fire escape?' he echoed in alarm. 'That's crazy! Send it to the laundry.'

'No, only the sheets. It's too expensive.'

'One of these days I shall come back to find you lying broken on the pavement.'

'I'll be careful,' I promised. 'But I do like my washing dried in the fresh air.'

'Fresh air?' He was still frowning. 'Covered in smuts! But you just take care. Do you hear me?'

'Yes, darling. It's really quite safe, for I never look down at the street. I look up at the sky, and the clouds don't make me giddy,' I explained, patiently.

'Do you kiss me, or do I stand here all night talking about your darn washing?' he complained.

So it had its moments of satisfaction, and not even Marie-Louise could spoil my enjoyment of Soho. It was a way of life, and I could not embrace it as Paul could, for language was a barrier, and my shyness was a barrier. But I watched, and listened, and shopped in the street market like all the other women who lived there.

Once again we had exchanged roles. Paul was happy and

confident. I was still nervous, anxious, crying too easily. While Paul spent his day in the midst of traffic – human and mechanical – I would walk in the parks every afternoon, searching for quiet paths, gazing longingly at the flower beds – thinking of my own small garden in Somerset, a garden I had created out of a wilderness. Paul never once mentioned the cottage, and neither did I, but I kept it safe in that secret part of me he could not reach. It is still there, small and safe, clothed in memory – my dream cottage. But for Paul it was a wasted period of time that his big, exciting world had already obliterated. Absorbed in the present, he looked neither back nor forward. I did both, with sad nostalgia for one and apprehension for the other.

He took me to Covent Garden and Sadler's Wells. We saw *Aida, Carmen* and *La Bohème.* Tears poured down his cheeks, while I sat unmoved and disenchanted by the lavish stage spectaculars. 'I still think the only way to enjoy opera is to lie in the arms of the beloved and listen to the wireless,' I told him, candidly.

And he shouted with laughter. 'Sweetheart, you're crazy! There is no comparison. This is *live* opera.'

I shook my stubborn head. 'It's too artificial – too many people screaming at the top of their voices. Take me to see a good film. Then you will see me cry!'

'Okay, my sweet. Next time we go to the movies,' he agreed.

But I had to breathe fresh air, to see trees and flowers, and I found all three in the London parks. In the tiny penthouse apartment I felt cramped and depressed. Some nights I woke stifled in the bed under the low, sloping roof, and would stand at the window, breathing the cool night air, searching the sky for stars. When I crept back to bed, Paul's arms would close around me, and I would bury my face in his warm, living flesh, feel the strong beat of his heart. He was tender and compassionate on these nights when I longed most desperately to be back in the country. He knew the longing was there, but it would pass, for I could always adapt myself to new conditions and a fresh environment.

But this time it was taking longer, for I was constantly aware of Marie-Louise listening at the door, or creeping up the fire escape to catch me unawares.

'Wash! Wash! No wonder you 'ave so much the 'eadache!' she would scold me, as I hung Paul's shirts over the line.

'My husband must have a clean shirt every day, Madame,' I told her, determinedly.

'Your *'usband?'* she scoffed. And her shrill, mocking laugh always brought tears to my eyes.

But the man at the helm of the ship called 'Trade Expeditions' was not the same man who cradled me in his arms at night, and dried my weak tears. I counted the hours, the minutes to his return, then hung over the banisters. The urgent need to be together was as strong as ever.

During this first Winter in London, with Paul out during the week, I got in touch with my former Editor, and wrote more short stories for women, and found several new markets for children's stories and travel articles. But all were poorly paid, and I had to wait from three to six months for payment. It served to give me back the confidence and independence I had lost with Marie-Louise, and the small cheques always seemed to arrive when my purse was empty.

At the end of three months not one of Paul's team of picked salesmen had brought back an order. I could sense their embarrassment every Friday night. Like Paul, they all were past middle-age, and their chances, competing with younger men, were slim. At the end of six months, these six men, who had become Paul's friends, collected their last cheques, had a good dinner and drinks to warm their cold hearts, then said goodbye. We never saw them again.

Paul's own engagement was extended for a further six months, when he kept on one typist in the London office and travelled around the country five days a week, in a last desperate attempt to save the sinking ship. He concentrated on the three spheres of which he had most knowledge - Textiles - Aircraft - Catering.

'My dear chap, you are flogging a dead horse!' he was told more than once by busy executives.

So, one lovely Spring evening, exactly a year after arriving in London, we were both invited to dine at the 'Caprice' with the gravely puzzled and disappointed creator of 'Trade Expeditions'. It was the end of his venture.

* * * * *

We were living now in a rather pretentious apartment in Kensington. A terrace of Georgian houses had been converted into flatlets, and during the last week of the six months' search for suitable accommodation, I chanced upon a vacancy at Number Fifteen – a vast room on the ground floor, with an embossed ceiling and four French windows. No bigger contrast could be imagined then between the cramped little penthouse in Soho and this palatial apartment in Kensington!

The two maiden ladies who owned the property collected the rents once a month with such an air of refinement that I had to put the money in an envelope to spare them embarrassment.

After the first introduction, Paul left them to me, and told me, quite candidly, that he missed his verbal battles with Marie-Louise, and found her noisy vulgarity more congenial than these genteel landladies of Kensington. But the tiny kitchenette at the far end of the room was a real joy, and I vowed never to share a kitchen again. In my haste to move, however, I had overlooked the fact that we would be spending the Winter here, and such a large room would be cold and need more heating. The meter was fed with shillings and would devour them like a monster in a frightening fashion. But Paul was still earning a good salary at 'Trade Expeditions', and was only home at weekends, so he was quite unconcerned, even faintly amused, at such consternation over a gas meter.

'Forget it, sweetheart. Get a good supply of shillings from the bank once a week, and keep warm,' said he.

But we moved from Soho in November, and I could see how he crouched over the fire that first morning, with the fog filtering through those four ill-fitting windows. I was shivering in my dressing-gown as I made tea and coffee, and went on shivering all the Winter.

With Kensington Gardens only a short distance away, I walked and walked to get warm, and also to keep fit. In a sense, I also missed the crowded little penthouse, and certainly it would have served us better in the Winter months.

We often went back to 'Rinaldi's' on Saturdays, and Paul still went to his favourite pub for a drink.

'A guy wants to drink in congenial company, my sweet. I feel like I belong over there,' he explained – and took a taxi back to Soho!

Coming back to that chilly apartment, after spending ten days at Christmas in Mother's small house with its coal fires, was most depressing, for it was one of those houses where tenants merely exchanged a polite 'good-morning' on the front steps. Unlike the penthouse in Soho, this room was soundproof, so the place seemed empty and deserted. I remember I lit the gas-fire and huddled over it, in my thick Winter coat, drinking tea, waiting for Paul who would take a taxi from London Airport. I sadly missed the warmth and colour of a house gaily decorated for the festive season, and the company of family and friends, that evening. I had a little niece now – Henry's daughter – dark-eyed and olive-skinned, like her brother. They were Latin-type children – children of the sun. They had no country tendencies, no roots in the soil. They were agile as monkeys, talented, creative. Henry's children were not fashioned in the same mould as Henry, so they surprised and delighted him with their lively individuality.

William's son was a forester – a sturdy, contented, happy soul, living alone in a caravan with a dog for company. He was still Mother's favourite, because he was the first grandchild, born of her own first child. There is something in a mother that responds to a first-born son, and the relationship is very precious.

Mary had fulfilled her early ambition to be a children's nurse, and her deep maternal instincts were satisfied in other people's babies. She was in charge of a day nursery. Babies and toddlers were dropped into her arms like parcels, at seven in the morning, and collected again in the early evening by harassed working mothers. When the babies arrived, they were unwashed, hungry, and fretful. When they left, they were clean and sweet-smelling, sleepy and satisfied. Such was the transformation one loving, intelligent woman, with two adolescent assistants, could contrive.

The war had only disturbed them superficially. Now they all were back in their proper environment – William at the bank, Henry at his engineering, Mary with her babies – all Mother's children, shaping their lives sensibly.

After the Trade Expedition finally collapsed, and Paul was looking for another job, my writing was shelved again, for his movements were erratic, and he often spent all day in our apartment, and went to Soho to meet his friends for a drink in the evening. He would write letters, 'phone the employment agency, cook a meal, smoke incessantly, and drink strong black coffee. I knew he would quickly succumb to the old depression, and frustration would embitter a mind suddenly deprived of responsibility and initiative.

'Kiss me! Come to bed, sweetheart!' This was forgetfulness, and the bar at Soho was forgetfulness. He needed both. I could feel his impatience in every nerve of that big strong body, and the tears swam in my eyes at the harshness of his voice.

'I do apologize. Forgive me, my sweet.' Then his cradling arms, his gentleness, his renewed determination to be tolerant. And later, – 'Put on your hat and coat. I am taking you to a movie!'

Now I knew we should not have moved from Soho, and that sharing a kitchen with Marie-Louise was not the ultimate torment. I had survived for six months, and she had not murdered me with one of her precious kitchen knives!

'Why do I make so many mistakes?' I asked myself. 'Why not give second, serious thought to every situation?'

We were both miserable in our cold palatial apartment. Spaciousness could never compensate for cosiness. Now that Paul had room to pace up and down, he wanted only to huddle over the fire.

'How come you fell for this mausoleum, my sweet, and moved us in so quickly?' he asked.

I shook my head sadly.

'Well, look around. We don't want to spend another Winter here.'

So I looked around in other areas, had a snack at Lyons, and Paul went off to Soho at mid-day, for he couldn't bear to be left alone in the apartment.

Once again I was faced with an alternative – of taking a job and upsetting Paul, or spending all the money I had managed to save during the year he was working at 'Trade Expeditions'. I wanted to work, and there was plenty of scope for a woman, but I remembered Paul's reactions at the cottage in 1946.

'If I can't earn enough to keep you at home, I may as well blow out my brains and have done with it!'

Such hot-headed threats frightened me, for he would not be the first bitterly frustrated man to end his life in a last terrible gesture of hopelessness. I knew instinctively that he had recently borrowed money, but he would not tell me because I was so averse to borrowing. How much had he borrowed and from whom, I wondered - how could he possibly repay a loan? Jacqueline's allowance was top priority every week, and I could see no end to it. It had seemed a mistake to travel by air to Ireland, and buy the girl expensive presents during that one short year of prosperity, for now he had to revert to the old means of travel, by train and boat, and cut the allowance to £5 weekly. It was no use to argue and protest, for this was Paul's responsibility, not mine. Yet it was there, like a bone of contention between us, all the time. Why hadn't he insisted on a Court Maintenance Order years ago, when their marriage was irretrievably broken? I could not understand or sympathize with such an unsatisfactory arrangement. That registered letter to Londonderry was pushed across the Post Office counter every week, and we both came away feeling cheated.

'Sweetheart, do me a favour - come over to Soho and collect me about three o'clock, for I guess it's getting pretty well impossible to tear myself away!' Paul confessed, with a wry smile one morning, as we kissed and parted.

I had moved to the Bayswater area in my search for furnished rooms, and travelled by bus or walked. But I had noticed for some time past that he was reluctant to tear himself away from the congenial company of the bar parlour, and it worried me. He was either spending money we could ill afford, or he was accepting drinks from too many people, and, knowing Paul, it was more likely to be the former. To walk out, after an hour, or even two or three hours, was a self-discipline he could not seem to practise without my assistance, yet I was reluctant, as always, to enter this little world of the bar parlour, still so exclusively male.

'Just walk straight in, my sweet, and tell me firmly, "Paul, it's time to come home." ' he instructed me.

'You would soon get a reputation as a hen-pecked husband!' I laughed.

'Oh, but all my friends in Soho know we are not married. That's why they are so anxious to meet you. They won't believe me when I tell them you don't drink or smoke.'

'Well, thanks for the information!' I choked indignantly, and bounced out of the room. Why couldn't he bring himself home? Why was he so strong in some ways, so weak in others? I sighed as I waited at the bus-stop that afternoon, for I was footsore and weary, after trekking around Bayswater all morning, and wanted only to sit on a bench in Kensington Gardens.

In a haze of smoke, I could see Paul seated at a table with a group of men, gesticulating with a glass of wine. He was talking with the old animation, his face alert and eager, his dark eyes glowing. I stood, hesitating, on the threshold, recognizing the man who sat there as the other half of the irate, chain-smoking companion of our Kensington apartment. How he loved an audience! He would never change. Then he caught my eye, gulped the wine, and spoke in a loud, clear voice.

'Gentlemen! You must excuse me. My sweetheart is waiting!'

All the men in his company turned their heads to look at me, and I backed out, blushing with embarrassment. Paul strode towards me, and whispered urgently, 'Please don't go. You don't have to drink if you don't want to, but just say hullo to my friends.' Then he wrapped a protective arm round my shoulders and took me back to the table. The seven or eight men stood up to greet me, smiling a welcome.

'Gentlemen! – my sweetheart!' Paul announced, and they all shook hands, and offered me chairs and drinks.

'No, thank you. I am not stopping – and I don't drink,' I told them, candidly.

Paul squeezed my shoulders. 'These guys wouldn't believe me!'

They looked me over with undisguised amusement.

'You seem to have tamed this old rascal, my dear!' said one.

They watched us curiously as we walked away, hand-in-hand. They were still standing, still staring, when we turned to wave.

Outside on the wet pavement, Paul stopped to kiss my mouth. 'Sweetheart, you were marvellous! I was so proud of you! Now I feel good. I feel like somebody just left me a million dollars!'

'What again?' I teased him.

Still gripping my hand, he waved the other at a passing taxi. 'Hey! Somebody stop that cab!' he yelled – dragged me down the street, and pushed me inside.

'Where are we going, darling, and why don't we take a bus?' I asked, breathlessly.

He was looking at his watch. 'Sadler's Wells – we've only missed half-an-hour of the matinée!' he told me extravagantly.

Sitting on the edge of the bed, early one morning, pouring a second cup of coffee for Paul, I saw him staring at my hair.

'It's grey,' he said, bleakly.

'My darling, you are not very observant. I was grey before we left the cottage!' I spoke lightly, for it did not bother me. 'All the women in our family are grey at forty. It must be worrying over the men they choose to marry!'

'It was so pretty – it's still pretty, but it's grey,' he sighed.

'I could get it dyed. Would you like a blonde, brunette or redhead?'

He frowned at my flippancy, for he was not in the mood for joking. 'Remember that day you turned up at Brown's Hotel with a permanent wave, looking like Shirley Temple?'

'I shall never forget it.'

'I was mad at you,' he reflected.

But I knew it was not only my grey head that saddened him to-day. He was starting his new job – as a commercial traveller. And I was waiting to tell him my own news before he left. It could not be told until he was actually starting work for fear of upsetting him. Another long period of unemployment had left us both emotionally exhausted, our nerves tense with waiting. His pride – his stupid pride – would be appeased only when he brought home his wages at the end of the month. He would peel the crisp bank notes from his wallet on to the table, smiling with proud satisfaction.

'Let me know if you want any more,' he would say.

'Yes, darling. Thank you very much, but I am sure I shall manage fine with this,' I had to answer. It could be £20. It could be less, or more, for it would depend on the commission. The wages were small, so a man was obliged to work hard to earn a living for himself and his family.

'You'll have to flog yourself, mate!' one of the firm's travellers had told him candidly, over a drink at the local. But he hadn't known Paul had two homes and two wives.

'Darling,' I began tentatively, – 'I think I have found the

answer to one of our problems in Bayswater. I have only taken it on a month's trial period, just in case.'

'In case what?' he snapped, instantly defensive.

'Well, you may not like it, and I expect I shall find a few snags.'

He was looking at me now with hard eyes. 'Well, go on,' he said, impatiently.

Suddenly my face crumpled, and I covered it with my hands, crying helplessly. 'I must *do* something. I am just wasting my time. I feel so useless - like - like a parasite. You must let me work - you *must,* you *must!'*

He set down the cup and pulled me into his arms. I had been on the verge of tears since he came back to tell me about the new job. Now I couldn't stop crying. All the mounting problems of our precarious existence flowed out of me, together with the sadness of Paul's inexorable descent down the ladder - a commercial traveller - what next? I was choked, inarticulate, but he understood. His shoulder was still strong, his arms loving, his voice coaxing, as to a child.

'Sweetheart, tell me what you want to do, where you want to go, and we will do it together. I swear I won't raise any more objections. From to-day you're the boss! I don't give a damn where we live, so long as we stay together. Don't give up now, my sweet. You've been so brave. I depend on you, I need you.'

'We need each other. I couldn't live without you. But I'm frightened, darling. I have a premonition something is going to happen to separate us,' I sobbed distraughtly.

'That's silly, sweetheart. Nothing in this world can separate us now,' he said convincingly. Then he gave me a clean handkerchief to blow my nose, and I saw he was smiling cheerfully again.

'Well, I'm ready, sweetie! When do we go some place else?' he demanded.

'Today - to an apartment house in Bayswater. We get a flat in the basement rent free, with free heating, in return for my services as a housekeeper.'

'Well, that sounds pretty good to me,' he said, without a second's hesitation.

And I knew he was going to keep his promise, and I should have no further objections about doing my share.

I picked my way carefully down the area steps. They were shiny with wet coal dust, and littered with scraps of decayed cabbage from the dustbins. The taxi-driver, a cheery Cockney, had carried down our boxes and heavy cases, and I was making my third journey down with what he politely called 'the clutter'.

'I'll take the big stuff, luv. You bring the clutter,' said he, with a wide grin. 'And watch yourself on these bloody steps,' he added. 'Lumme, what a dump! – not 'arf it ain't.' He whistled shrilly in the dark passage. 'Cor blimey, luv, it's 'ot as 'ell!'

A wave of suffocating heat hit us both between the eyes.

'My husband likes it stuffy. The last place was as cold as charity,' I told him.

'Nothing like a change, luv; 'e won't 'arf get scorched in this ruddy place. Tickled pink, I shouldn't wonder, when 'e comes 'ome to-night!'

'It's the boiler. It heats the water for the whole house,' I explained. 'And the bedroom is next door to the boiler room.'

'No need to turn on the 'eat then, luv. You got it all the time!' he grinned impishly.

I laughed at his coarse joke. He was boosting my morale. Had I made another dreadful mistake? What would Paul say to this sweltering basement? I threw open the windows, and a slight current of air stirred the dirty curtains.

There were three small rooms – a sitting-room, bedroom and scullery. We should use the bathroom on the ground floor, but there was a wash-basin in the bedroom.

'Would you like a cup of tea?' I asked my cheery companion, reluctant to part with him.

'No thanks. Can't stop. So long, luv!' He ran up the steps, and I was left alone at the scullery door, looking at the messy yard, the row of dustbins, and the clothes line. Could I make a home of this drab, stuffy basement? I sighed, put on the kettle, and made my first cup of tea, then I made a detailed tour of our new apartment, for I had had time only for a cursory glance when the former housekeeper showed me round.

The owner of the house was living in Dorset. The housekeeper let the rooms, collected rents, cleaned steps, stairs and bathrooms, and received a pound a week for these services, plus the basement flat. I had not mentioned the cleaning part of the contract to Paul, and I had already decided to clean the front steps by the light of the street lamp, before my darling husband or my tenants were awake! The stairs and bathrooms would be cleaned during the morning, when everyone had left the house.

'I shall manage,' I told myself decidedly.

I had been saying it all my life, and I was an echo of Mother, who, in turn, was an echo of her mother. Would she be horrified, disgusted, or reconciled, to see me here? Another new address, and a little more pretence, to cover up the plain truth, that every place was poorer than the last?

The windows were barred for security, and grimed with dirt, the gas-stove was sticky with grease, and a pile of rubbish on the bedroom floor suggested the last housekeeper had left in a hurry, and had intended to make a bonfire – in the bedroom, perhaps? The rooms were furnished with an odd collection of pieces that might have been bought at a junk shop.

'She was a dirty slut, that last housekeeper,' I told myself. 'It's poor, but it needn't be filthy.'

Even a clothes line in a yard full of dustbins was better than the last place, where tenants were not allowed to hang out so much as a handkerchief, for fear of spoiling the refinements of Kensington. There had been no washing problems at the hostel, or the cottage, only in London.

Soon I was sluicing the area steps with buckets of water, when a voice accosted me from above.

'Hey! You! – Are you the new housekeeper?'

I forced a weak smile to my grubby face.

'Oh, hullo, yes I am.'

'Well, you might come up and let me in. I've left my key upstairs.'

'Just a minute.'

It seemed easier to open the door to this irate tenant than to explain I was not on duty till the morrow, so I climbed the steep basement stairs, hurried down the passage, and opened the front door to a short, plump woman, loaded with shopping.

'Thanks,' she said, and walked past me. She hadn't asked my name, or told me hers. I was a nonentity here – a woman in the basement who collected rents and cleaned the steps. Paul would be a nonentity, too – the housekeeper's husband, coming down the area steps to the scullery door. I hadn't thought of it until that rude tenant pushed past me. Now I went slowly back down the basement stairs, and sank wearily on to the edge of the bed.

The mattress had been aired, and now the bed was made with our sheets and blankets, and covered with a plaid rug. I had washed, dried and ironed the chair covers and curtains – in the heat of the boiler room they were dry in an hour. The sitting-room table was spread with a blue check cloth, and a bunch of asters I had bought on the way from a street vendor looked gay and pretty in a blue jug. I liked the fresh smell of furniture polish, and now I could see the clean steps through the polished window.

Later in the day, my poor old darling would descend those steps to his new home. 'My poor old darling' – the thought was involuntary. For the first time, I saw him poor and old. The years that had turned my hair grey, and lined my face, had aged Paul. Only in Soho had I caught a glimpse of the man he used to be – gay, bold, arrogant.

When he came back to our basement home that first evening, I heard his dragging footsteps on the area steps. Then he pressed his face to the barred window, and we looked at each other for a long moment. The gas-fire glowed in the hearth, and a meal was laid on the table. The strong aroma of coffee was stronger than the hot smell of the coke boiler. He opened the door and came in.

'It's real homey, sweetheart,' he said with a tremulous smile.

But behind the smile, his face was pale and drawn, and his eyes were wet.

Paul had replied to an advertisement which read: 'Are you an energetic, enthusiastic, experienced salesman? – if so, we need you.'

He wasn't. He was a tired man, but he got the job, and there were fifty-seven applicants!

'I bluffed them,' he told me simply.

Now he was a 'representative' in the retail trade, and since all his customers could be found in a specified area of North London, he was unlikely to meet any of his Soho friends or pre-war associates. He would have to travel by bus and Underground, for no car was provided. With a basic salary of £500 a year, he would have to work hard to earn commission on orders. It was not only a matter of satisfying the old customers, but finding new ones. It was a big, expanding firm, with a young Sales Manager, and Paul had to prove his brash assertion, 'Sure, I can sell anything!' He would give all of himself, again - sell himself, because it was the only way he knew to do a job. He would drive himself too hard, need more drinks, more cigarettes, more black coffee, to sustain the pace. I could only listen, sympathetically, every evening, to the tale of his day's endeavours, smile at his bluffing and boasting, and praise his success. He was so pathetically anxious to impress that young Sales Manager, to prove that an older man could still beat the younger ones in open competitive markets. He knew what to say, and how to say it. There had never been a time when Paul was not selling himself to an audience - even an audience of one. I was his audience in the evening. 'I need you' was not only a physical need. I was the open mind into which he poured his success and failure, his fears and frustrations, his hopes for the future. For hope had not yet died. The spark could be kindled by the single small achievement of adding a new customer to his list.

'Another new customer to-day, my sweet!' he would tell me, with a gleam of triumph in those dark, searching eyes. 'Shall we go to a movie, or "Rinaldi's" for supper? We can afford a small little celebration.'

'Let's go to "Rinaldi's",' I would say, for then I would see the old Paul emerge from the taxi - shoulders squared, straightening his bow tie, the homburg hat swept off in greeting, the polite little bows, the warm hand-clasps with Rinaldi and his wife.

'And how is my good friend to-night?' Rinaldi would ask.

'Great! Marvellous!' A hoot of laughter, and his arm about my shoulders.

I watched the little drama enacted, choked with admiration, for I knew he would be on the verge of collapse when we were back in Bayswater. He would clutch my hand on the area steps, draw a gasping breath in the scullery, and sink exhausted into the armchair. He carried a little flask of brandy now.

'Why do you need a flask? Are you ill, my darling?' I asked him, anxiously, when I discovered it in his pocket.

'Not ill, my sweet - just tired,' he told me, and quickly changed the subject.

I was enjoying my own working routine, for a full, busy day

had always suited me. At the end of the month, the owner of the house seemed pleased when I telephoned to say I would stay on indefinitely. But he was certainly getting his 'pound of flesh' from a working housekeeper, for it was not only chores and rent collecting and letting rooms, but taking 'phone messages, paying the milkman, obliging tenants with shillings for their meters, changing library books, and drying wet clothes in the boiler room. I had only one strict rule – the basement was private – and I was fierce in enforcing it!

Paul came and went unnoticed, but the late evening was devoted to his comfort and leisure. We were often disturbed, however, with a plaintive appeal for a shilling from the top of the basement stairs, and Paul would frown, and threaten to tick them off for taking liberties.

'You spoil them, sweetheart, like you spoilt all the boys on Block Number Eight at the hostel,' he reminded me one evening.

'Only because I remember a time when I hadn't a shilling left for the gas meter at the end of the month, and dear Katie O'Brien never once refused to lend me one, till pay-day. I always get them back, darling.'

But he was impatient of the tenants' demands on me. 'You are not paid to do that. Why make yourself a slave?'

'Perhaps I like being a slave?'

'*My* slave – not that lot. I want you to myself,' he complained.

'You are my best beloved,' I would comfort him. If he fell asleep in the chair after supper, I would pick up a book, turn the pages, and remember nothing I had read, watching him like an over-anxious mother. When he slept, exhausted, I could see his eyes were ringed with dark shadows, his forehead creased with anxious lines, and his hands fell loose in an unconscious attitude of dejection. He was coughing a lot – 'a smoker's cough' he called it, but I knew it was the dust and fumes from the boiler.

'What shall I do? Where shall we go next?' I asked myself. Here I had work to do, and no rent to pay. What was the answer to this eternal problem of two homes and two wives? How did other men manage in similar circumstances? There must be so many couples like ourselves, who met during the war and couldn't bear to part when the war was over. For the sake of the child, we had been sacrificed, yet the sacrifice was built on the altar of our own weakness. Who could blame a child for her parents' mistakes? Hadn't we deprived her of one parent since she was a little girl of six? Now it was too late. She did not need a father. She was in love with a young man of twenty-five in the same theatrical touring company in which she had a small part, and she had written six pages of scrawled, enraptured description of her wonderful Richard. This, too, was hard to accept for a man like Paul.

'But she's only a baby,' he protested, reading aloud the letter one evening.

'She's not a baby. She is a grown-up young woman, in love for the first time,' I reminded him gently. But he clung to the little girl illusion as long as possible, visiting her when she was on tour, staying in hotels to be near her for a few days, and spending hours waiting for a glimpse of her, either on stage, or in the bar of the hotel. He did not go to Ireland any more, for Rosalinde was seldom at home, and providing Jacqueline received her weekly allowance of £5, she did not worry him. Two of his sisters had died in recent years, but it was so long since they met, their death hardly disturbed him. He was more concerned with my family than his own, and I always read aloud any letters I received from Mother, Mary or William. Henry did not write letters, but left it to his wife to answer mine.

Sitting in that basement room, reading their letters, I felt an outcast, permanently estranged from the family. But I could see no remedy, since my loyalties were no longer divided. 'I need you, sweetheart.' The others did not need me, and I had to feel this need, to give of myself, to be drained of everything but that one small seed of creativity – and that would never be drained. It was measureless, it had no depth or shape. You could not drain a well of thought and feeling, and inspiration. If I was saddened by circumstance, and shamed by people like Marie-Louise, I was still fundamentally happy and hopeful. It was a contradiction that could not be explained, for sorrow and joy walked together, side by side, and every day I met them both, for they were inseparable. I still could laugh at myself and weep for Paul. And now, at long last, I was relieved of the migraine that had troubled me since I was seventeen.

We still had our portable gramophone and we had collected quite a varied selection of records over the past ten years. Paul was still a confirmed opera addict, but my musical tastes had expanded to include Chopin, Beethoven and Rachmaninoff. I hadn't dared to put on a record with Marie-Louise so easily upset, and the chilling atmosphere of our last apartment had sent us out for our entertainment. Paul was obsessed by the urge to add more customers to his list. All the younger travellers owned cars, and had a petrol allowance. They could cover their territories quickly and easily.

'I took a taxi to-day. I was pushed for time,' he would tell me. But this he would pay for from his own pocket, for he could not include taxi fares on his expenses. The little flask was filled each morning from a bottle of brandy I kept in the cupboard.

'But I'm a darn good salesman – one of their best,' he boasted.

'Of course you are. They are lucky to have you.' So I boosted his morale. But I was not deceived. I knew him too well to be deceived. He was a very sick man.

The tenants were a mixed bunch, but the girls on the top floor used the place as a sort of transit camp, coming and going so quickly I hardly remembered their names. Bed-sitting-rooms were old-fashioned, they told me, and the new vogue was for four girls to share a flat and all the expenses. They usually asked my permission before inviting their boyfriends to a late-night party, but I couldn't keep an eye on them all the time, and the other tenants complained of meeting strange men in the bath-room!

'What does it matter? You are not responsible for their morals, only for their rents. They can all go to bed together, sweetie, so long as they leave us in peace in the basement!' said Paul, one evening, yawning expansively in the armchair.

Then a querulous voice called down the stairs – 'Mrs Taylor! Mrs Taylor! They haven't left my *Daily Mirror* again.'

'Get me a gun, and I'll shoot the lot of them!' Paul shouted.

'My poor darling. Shall we move from here?' I asked him. 'Shall we go some place else?'

He grinned at the American jargon. 'Sweetheart, I do apologize,' he said contritely – and we stayed.

Jacqueline always acknowledged her allowance in a brief, polite letter in which she mentioned Rosalinde's movements.

For some time past, only postcards had been received from the girl, and there were no more of the long, scrawled, affectionate letters to her father. I knew he was disappointed that she hadn't achieved very much in her stage career as yet, and was playing only minor roles. She lacked ambition and seemed perfectly happy in a second-rate touring company, probably because of Richard. Paul had no need to tell me she was very attractive, for I could see it for myself on the professional photographs taken for advertising.

He always came back from his meetings with her very quiet and subdued, for the early loving intimacy of father and daughter would never be recaptured. They spoke a different language, this young, post-war generation, and she blew in with her friends, pecked his cheek, perched on a stool in the bar, and sipped Dubonnet. Jacqueline had apparently accepted her new status more sensibly than Paul, and even allowed herself to be called 'Jackie'. Paul was deeply shocked at such a liberty, but his daughter had laughed and called him a 'dear old-fashioned fuddy-duddy'.

'I reckon I've missed out somewhere,' he told me, sadly.

But now, one Saturday morning, Paul was surprised by a long letter from his wife and he scanned the pages anxiously.

'It's Rosalinde. They've had a row over Richard. Her mother thinks he is a bad influence, and she wants me to go over to sort it out. The company is playing in Belfast for four weeks.'

I sighed with exasperation. We had planned to see a film and have supper at 'Rinaldi's' to celebrate our Anniversary – the Anniversary of our meeting that lovely evening in May, 1942. It was the one day in the year I never allowed Paul to forget, for every woman needs a special day to celebrate, and he paid so little attention to birthdays and Christmas. I had always received a bouquet of flowers, and we exchanged cards with sentimental verses.

'Sweetheart, I must go,' he said – and all thought of a celebration was swept aside. This keen disappointment and his casual indifference was too much for me.

'Rosalinde! Rosalinde!' I choked indignantly. 'It's always the same old story. It will never be any different. What good can you do? She is not a child any more. Let her alone. Why should you, or her mother for that matter, have the audacity to suggest that her boyfriend is a bad influence? What have you done, either of you, to preserve the sanctity of marriage?

I am asking you, Paul. Why should your daughter respect your wishes, or ask your advice? Don't be such a damned hypocrite! Give me one good reason why your daughter should benefit from your visit?'

He looked at me in amazement, then his own anger flared, as I knew it would. 'For God's sake, Sarah, must we go over it all again? I thought you were reconciled to the fact, years ago, that I have to go when my daughter needs me?'

'She doesn't need you any more – and as for being reconciled,' I laughed mirthlessly, 'I shall never be reconciled, never!'

We glared at each other defiantly, torn apart by a problem I had not been able to solve – the jealousy I could not cure. In all the years we had lived together, I had shed more tears over his child than any other person. Of course it was unreasonable, but an angry exchange of words and bitter tears had only hardened the core of jealousy I felt for this lovely, innocent child. Perhaps Paul was partly to blame in not reversing the situation, to look at it with my eyes, not his own, but he was incapable of doing this.

'Well, come along then! If you must go, get started!' I was nagging him now, like a fishwife. 'You haven't any time to spare for hanging around here! I suppose you intend to fly over and back to-morrow night? You will find some money in that red tea caddy – and don't spend it all! Clean shirt and pyjamas in the bottom drawer. Turn off the gas-fire before you go. Goodbye, Paul.'

I pecked his cheek, buttoned up my overall, and ran upstairs to clean the bathrooms, with angry tears streaming down my cheeks.

I spent two of the longest and most miserable days I had ever known in all our time together. What had I done? How could I let him go away in such a temper? I was bitterly ashamed at my own childishness. He was not only anxious, but sick. I had made no coffee, and given him no sandwiches for the long journey. Now I wept afresh, in the big, lonely bed on Saturday night, listening to the happy revellers walking past on the pavement overhead, and the tenants coming in and out the front door. It was mean of me. I did not recognize myself with such meanness. Just before midnight on Sunday, I heard the taxi grind to a halt, and flew to the door. The light from the scullery shone on the broad figure descending the steps. He had taken only a brief-case, and he was carrying a large bouquet. He dropped the case and the flowers on the copper, gasped 'Sweetheart!' and folded his arms around me.

'I'm sorry, darling. Can you forgive me?' I was sobbing contritely.

'Forgive you?' He seemed puzzled. Then his hands gripped my shoulders, and a slow grin spread over his pallid face. 'My, my, you were mad at me, and I was mad at you. We must be crazy at our age. And you were right, my sweet. You were so right. I spent a lot of money, and did a hell of a lot of talking, but for all the good I've done, I could have stayed right here.' Then he handed me the flowers, and said quietly, 'Happy Anniversary, sweetheart. I hadn't forgotten. Tomorrow night we go to the movies, and have a late supper at "Rinaldi's". Bless you! What should I do without you? It's just the two of us now. Could I have a cup of coffee and a fried egg?'

The glow of the gas-fire and the pink-shaded light disguised the defects of the basement sitting-room. I peeled off his overcoat, and pushed him into the armchair. There were flowers on the table, and a small pile of clean shirts. He spread his hands, glancing about the room.

'It's so homey. I guess I don't deserve it.'

'I love you,' I said, – 'I love you very much,' – and went back to the scullery to make coffee and fry some eggs.

'Now, tell me what happened?'

He was sipping his third cup of coffee, smoking a cigarette, completely relaxed. And he told me how he had taken a taxi from the airport to the address Jacqueline had given him, and found Rosalinde and Richard living together in a furnished room, over a chemist shop. They hadn't expected him that day, of course, but they must have known he would soon be calling on them. The door on the first landing stood wide open, and Rosalinde was frying sausages in a pan over a gas-stove. She had a tiny apron over her dress, and her hair tied back with a ribbon. She looked a child, but she wasn't a child, and although her face flushed when Paul spoke to her from the doorway, her voice was calm when she answered him.

'Hello, darling,' he said.

And she looked up from the pan to say, 'Hello, Daddy.'

A young man was sitting on the edge of the table, smoking

a pipe. He slid to the floor, removed the pipe, and grinned boyishly. He was tall and blond, very casual.

'This is Richard,' said Rosalinde, carefully turning the sausages in the pan.

'How do you do, sir?' Paul's hand was gripped, and probably for the first time in his life he could think of nothing to say.

'Shall I take your coat and hat? Won't you sit down? I'll get you a drink.'

'Thank you, Richard.'

It was a Dubonnet. They seemed to like Dubonnet. He sat in the only armchair, and watched his daughter fork the sausages on to a plate, put the plate in the oven, and fill the pan with mushrooms. Last of all, she fried the tomatoes.

'We have two shows tonight, Daddy. So we need a good supper,' she explained, – 'but there is plenty for three,' she added, and smiled at him as though he were a child, and she his mother.

'Your mother was anxious about you. That's why I'm here,' he told her.

'Yes, I'm sorry,' was all she said.

It was so totally different from what he had expected. He was prepared for a scene, for her mother made a scene over everything that annoyed or upset her. But the excitable girl he had seen with her friends in the hotel bars during the past two years was not the girl he saw now. She was quiet and calm, completely at ease, and so was Richard. The glances that passed between them, and the socks and shirts hanging on a string line across the open window, told Paul all he wanted to know. They were in love, and they were living together.

Still busy with the frying pan, Rosalinde turned her head to say, 'Richard's waiting for a divorce. His wife went off with another man. – Can you eat three sausages, Daddy?'

'Two,' he said.

'We are terribly in love, aren't we, darling?' she appealed to Richard, and he echoed, 'Terribly.'

He was spreading a clean cloth on the table, and setting places for three. She began to serve up the meal. The room was spotlessly clean and shining. There were flowers in a blue jug. Before she put the plates on the table, Rosalinde spoke again, as though she were anxious to have everything explained before they ate. She stood there, a plate in each hand, her face flushed from the heat of the stove, and told her father, quietly, 'You see, Daddy, we knew you would understand. After all, you live with the person you love, don't you? Poor Daddy, don't look so shattered. I've known it for ages and ages. I think you were absolutely right to make another life for yourself if you didn't love Mother.' Then she paused, and added gently, 'I'm expecting a baby. You won't mind being a grandfather, will you, Daddy?'

* * * * *

Paul had been burning with fever all night, with a pain in his chest that frightened him, for he had never known physical pain.

'What's wrong with me?' he croaked, as the spasms clutched at his chest.

'I don't know, my darling. But we will soon find out. I shall 'phone the doctor early.'

I tried to keep the anxiety out of my voice, for now he wanted to lean on me, and it was my shoulder that cradled his hot head when the pillow was damp with sweat.

Since he came back from Belfast, three months ago, I had noticed a gradual deterioration in his health and energy, and the cough had worsened. It seemed he had at last realized he was no longer important to his daughter, and the efforts he had made to impress her all through the years of childhood and adolescence had suddenly been proved worthless and unnecessary. She had not wanted his money, or the 'extras' that his money had provided. It was her mother who insisted on music and dancing lessons, horse riding and ice-skating.

'Your father will pay,' was quoted so often that the child accepted the fact without question, as all children do. If she had known of his straitened circumstances since the war, or that he borrowed money on more than one occasion to pay for the journey to Ireland, the presents, and the treats she naturally expected, she would probably have been quite understanding and sympathetic. If the truth had been faced and spoken through the years, instead of so many lies, so much pretence, the happy relationship between father and daughter may have been closer, more lasting. It saddened him to know it was too late, and his adored daughter had found happiness, not in a luxury home, but in cheap lodgings, with the boy she loved.

For me, there had been no pretence, no need to lie, no need to hide his real self under the cloak of the public image. I probably knew Paul better than anyone had ever known him – the Jekyll and the Hyde – for I loved them both. I do not know why he accepted me, as I accepted him, without question, exactly as we happened to be at that moment of meeting.

'Here I am. Take me and love me for what I am. Don't ask me to be any different.' This is what we said to each other, silently, as our eyes and hands met, and held. There was no need to speak, when all could be said without words. Fundamentally, we were the same two people – separate, yet together, individual, yet partnered – necessary to each other's very existence, yet able to walk alone, to part and come together again.

'I am your man. You are my woman,' Paul said to me that day, but it was his heart that spoke, and my heart that answered.

'My poor darling.' I cradled his head on my shoulder, and fed him with sips of brandy.

'My job? – will you 'phone the office?' He was frowning with anxiety.

'Of course. Don't worry. It will be all right.'

'I feel like somebody is sticking a knife in my chest.'

'It will soon be better. The doctor will give you an injection.'

For the first time he did not reach for a cigarette when he smelled the strong aroma of coffee. For the first time he pushed the coffee away.

'It tastes queer. Would you get me a drink of water.'

'Water?' If Paul was asking for water he was really ill.

He was a busy doctor, and couldn't call until after surgery, he explained kindly, but asked about the symptoms, and advised, 'Keep the patient warm, and don't bother him with food. I'll be along later.'

Paul smiled weakly when I repeated these instructions. 'It couldn't be any hotter in hell,' he whispered. 'Would you open the window, wide.'

'My darling, you really are sick – water and fresh air!' I teased him lovingly.

The tenants' demands seemed paltry and irritating that morning, and my mind was far removed from the extra pint of milk, the reminder that Miss Brown liked to borrow the hoover on Wednesday, and Mr Ferguson had lost two collars at the laundry.

Doctor Lang was a puny, insignificant little man, but his sudden, radiant smile as he came into the room warmed my heart, and steadied my nerves.

'Hello, old chap! What's the trouble?' He took Paul's wrist and studied his face attentively. Then he reached for the stethoscope in his bag, and examined his chest and back. I had to hold Paul upright, for he was already weakened by pain. Then he lay back, panting, and asked, 'What's the verdict, Doc? Break it gently.'

'Pleurisy.'

'Pleurisy?' I gasped.

The doctor turned his head to look at me. 'It's not nearly as serious as it sounds. We treat it with penicillin injections these days. I shall call in twice a day to see your husband, until I am satisfied the inflammation has cleared. The real cure is rest. Three weeks, at least, in bed. Keep that door closed, and the window open. These old-fashioned coke boilers are no good to people with weak chests. What have you been doing to yourself, old chap?' he asked, kindly, sitting on the edge of the bed. 'A body is not a machine, you know.'

Paul was grinning cheerfully, and already his breathing seemed easier, for he was relieved to have the pain explained. 'Can we offer you a drink, Doc? Or a cup of tea?'

'Neither, thanks. Can't stop! But we will have a drink together when we have cleared up that inflammation. That's a promise. In the meantime, no smoking, and plenty of fluids – non-alcoholic!' he laughed. Then he clasped Paul's hand, and followed me to the scullery. 'I shouldn't worry too much, Mrs Taylor. I am sure your husband has an iron constitution. But that filthy boiler is not doing his chest and lungs any good – or yours, for that matter. I should advise you to get out of here as soon as you can manage it,' he told me.

'Thank you, doctor. I will.'

He ran up the steps, and I went back to Paul.

'You heard what he said. It's not serious,' he croaked.

'You mustn't talk, darling. I will make you a jug of lemonade, and leave it here, then you can help yourself while I do my chores upstairs.'

'Lemonade?' he shuddered, but he was too weak and ill to protest, and watched me removing cigarettes, wine and brandy from the room, with a twisted smile. As I sponged his face, he muttered, 'Three weeks in bed, and a week's convalescence. Will they wait a month for me at the firm?'

With this nagging worry on his mind, he could not relax, so I decided to go and see his boss instead of 'phoning, and he gave me the address of the head office at Wembley.

'Try to get some sleep while I'm away. You didn't get a wink last night,' I coaxed.

'Neither did you.' He was pleased that I had decided to see the boss and explain the position. Paul's weakness and dependence had strengthened me, and I was prepared to tackle half-a-dozen bosses! Latent maternity was stirring in my empty arms. I wanted to hold him, to comfort him. I was his mother now, and he was my child. All passion was spent, and he looked at me now not with the eyes of a lover, or even a husband, but with the puzzled eyes of a helpless child, waiting to be told what to do.

I was away for nearly three hours, travelling by Underground and bus, for I dare not spend money on taxis. Pressing an anxious face to the barred window, I could see Paul's head on the pillow. Was he sleeping? I hurried to the bedroom, eager, to tell him the good news. His eyes, heavy with sleep, were fastened on the door, and his lashes were wet. I kissed him gently, and asked, 'You haven't slept?'

He shook his head on the pillow. 'What did he say?'

'It's all right. You are not to worry. Your job is safe for a month on full pay, and the commission due to you, I have here in my bag. The boss said you were an asset to the firm, and they didn't want to lose you. "Your husband is a super-salesman, Mrs Taylor" – that's what he told me, Paul. And I agreed with him. "My husband could sell the English Channel to a Frenchman!" I said.'

Paul tried to laugh, but choked on a cough. I could see the relief in his eyes. 'I could drink a cup of tea if you are making one,' he said.

'Tea?' I echoed.

But when I came back with the teapot, he was sound asleep.

'I have found us a nice bed-sitting-room in Notting Hill, so we shall be leaving here at the end of the month,' I told Paul, a fortnight later.

'Okay,' he said, and turned over a page of one of the detective novels I had borrowed from the public library. The penicillin had dispersed the inflammation, but left him very weak and depressed.

'Did you post the letter?' he asked me on Thursday, and there was no need to ask which letter.

'Yes, I posted it.'

'Thanks,' was all he said, but it was enough. There would be no more protests, no more bitterness. For Paul's sake that letter must be posted.

The doctor called on his last visit, had the promised drink, shook hands with both of us, and wished us good luck in the new lodgings. When he ran up the area steps for the last time, we felt we had lost a friend.

The house in Notting Hill was one of a terrace condemned by the local housing authorities, so the rents were low. The walls at both ends of the terrace were propped with massive posts, apparently holding it together since a landmine had demolished the surrounding estate during the first year of the war. Nobody paid any heed, however, to this small indication of probable collapse, and all the houses were swarming with families. A dusty laurel hedge surrounded a small patch of soil, on which a cat was scratching the day I arrived, by taxi, and hurried inside with our few belongings. The linoleum in the passage was clean and polished, and a red geranium made a splash of colour on the hall-stand.

I had reserved the front room on the ground floor. Paul had left for work that morning, and all day I was anxiously awaiting his return to our new lodgings, for he looked so pale and shrunken in his heavy overcoat as he climbed the area steps for the last time, and turned at the top to smile bravely, lift a hand in salute. I had given him money, and made him promise to take a taxi from the Underground station, not to stand about waiting for buses. Since his illness, he would have nothing to do with money, and handed it over to me with the announcement, 'You're the boss! I guess you can manage it better than I can. I can't be bothered with money any more. Just hand me out a couple of pounds every morning to cover my expenses, and I'm not buying any more drinks for all those sponging guys in Soho. If I want a drink, I will have it at home.'

But this surprising decision gave me no pleasure or satisfaction, for it was so unlike Paul, and the main reason for meeting his associates in a bar parlour was to enjoy their company and gather an audience about him. He was still a very sick man, I thought, if this gregarious appetite no longer had to be fed.

So a fresh bottle of brandy, and a bottle of Beaujolais adorned the top of the chest of drawers. The gramophone and records were piled on a small bamboo table, clean curtains were drawn across the window, a meal was laid on a check cloth, and the brass jug filled with a bunch of bright yellow chrysanthemums. Family photographs adorned the mantelpiece, and coffee was brewing. The cooking equipment was reduced to two gas-rings in the hearth, but I had managed to cook a rabbit stew, and it smelt quite savoury.

Searching for two nails on the green distempered walls, I hung Paul's little crucifix on one, and the other awaited the homburg hat. When I heard his heavy footsteps in the passage, I opened the door, cuddled him, and said, cheerfully, 'Welcome home, Paul!'

He kissed me, but said nothing. I could see his shadowed eyes travelling round the room, recognizing all the familiar objects, while I stripped off his overcoat, and hung the hat on the nail.

'Some place to hang my hat and you, sweetheart. That's all I need,' he would say. But he didn't. His face was stricken. I pushed him into the sagging armchair, and he was weeping uncontrollably. Tearing sobs shook his whole body. I knelt on the floor and folded my arms around him, choked with dismay and compassion.

'My darling, oh, my poor darling.'

Only once in my life had I seen a strong man weep in this way. I was a child, then, and I had never forgotten it. It was quickly over, and he was emptied of the agony of so much disillusion and disappointment. Pain had weakened him, and the discovery that he could no longer boast he was strong as a lion.

Then he lifted his head and squared his shoulders.

'I do apologize, my sweet. That was unforgivable when you

had worked all day on this place, to make it homey,' he said earnestly.

I knelt there, stroking his face, far more disturbed by this storm of weeping than the doctor's verdict of pleurisy. He kissed me and reminded me gently, 'I'm parched for that coffee.'

'Yes, of course, I'll get it.' My hands trembled over the pouring, and I was so shocked and stunned, he served the meal for both of us. Then we lay on the bed and slept, exhausted, for several hours.

I awoke to the touch of Paul's caressing hands on my breast, and his voice whispering, 'Sweetheart, I want you.'

I slid off the bed, and he began to undress me with the old sensual pleasure. It did not seem to matter now that this was another strange room, in a strange house, and our few pathetic little possessions were scattered around us. He was asking me for another chance to prove his virility, to forget the shattering experience of his terrible weeping.

'Do what you will with me tonight, my love,' I told him, smiling into his dark, shadowed eyes.

The old intensity was flowing over him, and I could feel the excitement in his racing pulses as his hands slid over my breasts and stomach, and held my thighs in a warm, possessive grasp. I took his face between my hands, and we knelt there for a long moment on the hearth rug, mouth clinging to mouth. Then all tenderness was lost in his thrusting tongue, and trembling loins. I was not his mother tonight, and he was not my child. For the last time he was the lover I had known in those early years – masterful, demanding. But intuition had already warned me he was desperately afraid of losing his virility, and his weakened body seemed to be struggling to contain the passion he could not control. Tonight, for the last time, I was completely enslaved by his sensuality.

'Sweetheart, I swear I shall die in your arms!' he gasped, as he lifted me on to the bed.

Would to God he had died in my arms that night, and been spared the suffering of the following two years.

I took a job as a daily nursemaid at one of the luxury flats on the Bayswater Road. It was a regular routine, six days a week, in all kinds of weather, for the mother of the three small children was a fanatic for Fresh Air!

I took the children to the park in the morning – the baby in a pram, the others on tricycles, then back to the flat to give them their dinner, an hour's rest while I did their washing and ironing, then back to the park, home to tea, baths, and bed. It never varied, but it suited me, and it seemed to suit the children, for they were still at an age when change was unwelcome.

'I saw you from the top of a bus today. A policeman was holding up the traffic and you were crossing the road with the pram, and the kids on their bikes,' Paul told me one evening, as I shook off the raindrops in the passage.

He was back before me most days, and would light the gas fire and have the kettle boiling.

'Only three things keep me ticking over all day – black coffee, sips of brandy, and coming back to you!' he confessed, with a scornful laugh at his own weakness. How much longer could he carry on with his job, I wondered. How soon would he collapse? His strong, heavy body was shrinking, his face was gaunt and hollow-eyed, but he was still driving himself relentlessly round the territory, to get the orders for the firm, though most days he was obliged to take a taxi by late afternoon. The pain in his chest had developed again and couldn't be blamed on the boiler. Sometimes, when I came in from my own work, I would see he was in pain, and I would lie on the bed and unbutton my blouse. He would suckle my breast till the pain eased, for now I was his mother again, and he was my child. He had nearly travelled the full cycle of life, but I was still expecting a miracle. I always expected a miracle, even in the face of disaster, and I would not anticipate Death.

We moved out of our lodgings in Notting Hill when the demolition squad moved in! I found us another ground floor room in the Paddington area. Over our heads, four lively Australian lads jumped and capered, and on our first Saturday in our new lodgings, they had a party to welcome a fifth boy who had joined them. We heard the girls arrive about nine o'clock, and by one o'clock on Sunday morning, driven mad by their noise and the thumping of feet on the ceiling, – I went upstairs to remind them my husband was ill, and would they please be quiet. 'It's Sunday,' I added unnecessarily.

The tall, lanky youth looked me over – he saw a faded little woman in a faded dressing-gown, and shrugged indifferently. My voice was sharp and my nerves ragged.

'Sorry, but the party's just getting nicely under way,' he drawled. 'And Sunday's as good a day as any to throw a party, for we don't have to work,' he added reasonably and closed the door.

'They've got no manners at all, these Australians!' I told Paul, indignantly, creeping back under the blankets.

The next week we moved for the last time, to Harrow Road.

Paul didn't see much of our new lodgings, for the very first night our friend, Doctor Lang, was hastily summoned by telephone.

'A nasty experience – a haemorrhage – and rather frightening. I'm sorry, old chap, but I had a feeling we should be meeting again,' he told Paul soothingly. Then he patted my hand. 'Don't worry, my dear. Your husband has an iron constitution, even if he has lost a lot of weight. He'll pull through. Keep him quiet and warm. I'll 'phone for an ambulance. We must get him into hospital. Just pack a small case, will you?'

Mechanically, I opened the drawers, and Paul watched me dispassionately from the bed.

Doctor Lang put his head round the door. 'They will be collecting you in half-an-hour. Okay?'

'Okay, Doc,' Paul whispered.

I sat down to wait, holding his hand. There was nothing left to say. We were both so shocked. Still clutching his hand, I sat with him in the ambulance. They left me standing alone in the long, empty corridor at three o'clock in the morning, and wheeled him away on a trolley. Then, at last, he found his voice, and called out cheerfully, 'Keep smiling, sweetheart!'

I called, 'I will – goodbye, darling.' Then he was gone. He was no longer my lover, husband or child, but just a broken body, to be mended in a big London hospital.

I was not present when the tall, distinguished man at the bedside told Paul, conversationally, 'Well, Mr Taylor, we have removed one of your lungs.'

'You've got a bloody nerve!' said Paul, testily – and the surgeon laughed. Sister blushed and shook her head reprovingly.

'I want to see my sweetheart,' Paul told her, as she moved away.

'You must wait until the visiting hour, Mr Taylor. You are not on the danger list,' she reminded him.

'Visiting hour?' He looked puzzled, for he was not yet acquainted with hospital rules and regulations.

'Can't a guy see his own wife when he wants?'

'Certainly not!' she snapped.

Then he grinned and capitulated. 'Okay, Sister. I guess you're the boss around here.'

I heard all about it from the staff nurse, that first evening, as I hurried towards the men's surgical ward – it was forty interminable hours since I had left him at the hospital.

'Your husband is going to be a wonderful patient, Mrs Taylor. He is so amusing. We need cheering up in this ward. I nearly died when he swore at the surgeon!' she giggled.

'I quite like it here, sweetie,' Paul told me complacently. 'But Sister says I have to behave myself. Surely a guy has a right to say just one small little swear word when he discovers he has been left with only one lung?'

'My poor darling. How will you manage with only one lung?'

'I shall manage fine. It's just a question of breathing properly. Sister says I shall be starting on the breathing exercises tomorrow.'

Already, I noticed, he was becoming hospitalized, and quoting Sister as the supreme authority. But he was more casual over losing a lung than losing a tooth at the dentist! Should I ever really know this man of mine, I wondered. I thought I knew him, but now, again, he surprised me.

'Shall I tell you something else, my sweet?' he was saying, eagerly. 'I've got three pints of new blood in my veins!' He grinned at my incredulous face.

'You don't look any different yet.'

'Oh, but I feel different. I feel marvellous!' he insisted.

'It's only half-an-hour for visiting in the evening. Aren't they mean?' I was clutching his hand, and the precious minutes were ticking away.

'Two hours on Sunday afternoon,' he reminded me, and seemed quite content with the arrangement.

It was so lonely in that crowded lodging house on the Harrow Road – far more lonely than an isolated cottage in the country. Nobody bothered with me, or asked about Paul. Perhaps the other tenants were not even aware that he had been taken away to hospital that first night.

When the young nurse rang the bell for visitors to leave, we clung together for a moment, then I walked away down the long ward, and turned to smile and wave in the doorway. He was smiling cheerfully, and raised a hand in salute.

During that first interminable week, I seemed to belong to nobody and had no place in the world at all. Lost and lonely, I was looking for another job, for my little family had moved away. I had to earn money and pass the time till Paul came back. I think I was right in assuming that Paul's apparent unconcern for me was pure relief at finding himself in a warm, comfortable place, where he hadn't to make any effort at all. Completely in the hands of doctors and nurses, with a good audience, he was lively and happy again, drawing attention to himself with an affected American accent. I noticed he was calling the nurse 'Honey' – Sister was 'swell' and he was exclaiming 'Gee' and pretending surprise that an elevator was called a lift!

'Darling, you're a bit of a hoaxer,' I teased him affectionately.

What did it matter? He was Sister's blue-eyed boy, and Rosie, the Cockney char, told me my husband was a 'proper scream'. No, Paul was not worried, but I was sick with anxiety. Supposing he couldn't work again? How should we live on my small wages? – and find £5 every Thursday afternoon for that registered envelope?

'Should I have written to Ireland?' I asked Paul, one evening.

'No need to worry, my sweet. I will write myself if you bring me some paper and envelopes.'

'What shall you tell her?'

'That I have had a minor operation.'

'Will she come over to see you?'

He shook his head, decidedly. 'No need to worry,' he repeated, and changed the subject quickly. 'What have you been doing with yourself all the week?'

'I have been to see your boss,' I said, guardedly – and waited for his reaction.

'How come you were not going to mention it?' he teased me playfully. I could see he was still completely relaxed, and not likely to start a heated argument. 'I'm listening. Go ahead,' he prompted.

'First I saw your doctor – the young one, on the wards this morning. I asked him to tell me, truthfully, how long it would be before you were fit for work. He asked what kind of work, and I explained about the travelling. "Three months", he said, quite definitely. So now we know, we can make our plans accordingly, can't we?'

Paul nodded, and repeated, 'Go on, I'm listening.'

I had all his attention now. 'Then I went to see your boss. He was very kind, and most concerned about you. He sent his regards and best wishes. I had to be honest with him, Paul, about the three months.'

'Sure.' He patted my hand approvingly.

I took a deep breath, and rushed on regardless – 'Your boss asked me if I would carry on your job, temporarily, for he didn't want you to lose any of your good customers. The salary will be paid direct to you, and I shall be entitled to the commission. You don't mind, darling?' I asked, doubtfully.

'Mind? It's marvellous! What a woman! What a wife!' he shouted excitedly – and a titter of amusement ran round the ward.

'I'm to start next week. But now I'm getting butterflies in the stomach. Paul, supposing I bungle the orders and lose customers?'

'What *I* can do, *you* can do,' he reminded me. 'Tomorrow we will work out the details, and I will have a list of my customers ready. They will be tickled pink, I shouldn't wonder, and you will be piling up the commission!' he chuckled. 'Sweetheart, I'm real proud of you. I shall broadcast it all round the ward after you've gone.'

He kissed me goodbye as the visitors' bell tinkled.

'Don't forget you've got a reputation to keep alive – Paul Taylor could sell the English Channel to a Frenchman!'

'That's what worries me!' I retorted, and gave him a parting hug.

Some five or six weeks later, Paul told me, quietly,

'Sweetheart, I am being discharged on Friday, and I have to be transferred to out-patients.'

He was suddenly serious and anxious.

'Darling! That's wonderful! I'll hang out the flags,' I exclaimed excitedly.

'I'm scared,' he whispered.

'It will be all right. We shall manage.' I folded his hand in mine and smiled reassuringly at his bleak face.

Twelve months had passed. Paul was brought 'home' by ambulance, and carried upstairs. He was taken to 'out-patients' for a check up once a month, and our dear Doctor Lang called in every Sunday morning for a drink and a chat. He always left a few pills, though he knew Paul would refuse to take them.

In this small bed-sitting-room, the double bed was pushed under the window, and Paul, propped on pillows, could see out. But the view, of roofs and chimneys, was often obstructed by wet garments flapping on the clothes line I had tied across the outside of the window.

As his body died, so died his spirit, for the one was indivisible from the other. The body had always been important to Paul. He had loved his big, healthy body, loved to boast he was as strong as a lion, loved to possess me. Now he looked at the shrunken flesh and found it repulsive. Bitterness clouded his mind. All emotion was dead, and with it all feeling for me, as a woman and wife. He was drowned in self-pity - querulous and demanding as an old man. And he was draining me of energy, of love, of compassion. I still hoped for a miracle. He was scornful now of my perpetual optimism, scornful of my tenderness, as I washed him, from top to toe each day before I left for work. There was no alternative but to leave him alone for hours - with detective novels, a glass of wine, the brandy, and a dainty sandwich he seldom ate, for he had no appetite. The brandy soothed him, and he probably slept for part of the day, for we had disturbed nights.

Since he would not allow me to write to Jacqueline, and insisted her usual allowance must be sent every week, it had to be done his way, to the end of the chapter. But the boss allowed me to please myself over the customers, and to use my discretion over those who could safely be left without a visit.

I managed to get back by four o'clock, when I cooked a light meal for the two of us of chicken or fish – on a gas stove behind a screen.

'How come you can still bear to look at me – a skeleton?' Paul asked me one morning, as I washed him.

'I love you, my darling.'

'Love?' he jeered – 'Pity is all you feel for me now – pity! It was a mistake – a colossal mistake – the biggest mistake I ever made in my whole life. Go on! Tell me I'm wrong. I'm listening. Sure, I'm listening. I guess I've got to listen, stuck in this bloody bed! There is no place else, is there? – only this dump you call home!'

'Don't! Don't!' I pleaded, tears streaming down my face. 'It's not true. It was not a mistake.'

He turned his face to the wall and closed his eyes.

I saw the first crocuses of another Spring, the day he died – a cluster of purple and gold on a patch of dusty soil in the Harrow Road. I stood and stared at this small miracle, then hurried back to tell Paul.

'Crocuses?' he repeated, 'not bluebells? – Sweetheart – I – do – apologize.'

4

Epilogue

'Oh God, whose nature is ever to show mercy and forbearance, we humbly entreat Thee for the soul of Thy servant, Paul, who, at Thy bidding, has today departed from the world. Do not deliver him into the enemy's hands, or put him out of mind for ever, but with Thy Holy Angels, welcome him and lead him home to Paradise.'

I fastened my eyes on the one familiar face – the grave young face of Father O'Brien. I felt his candid eyes searching mine – searching my soul – to find an answer in me, the woman who had loved this man. But he saw only a vague shadow in the back pew of the church, without substance. I fastened my heavy, tearless eyes on his face, because he alone in this church had once been aware of me as a person, but for these others, I had no existence. His ears had heard the last confession, his young hands blessed Paul's emaciated body, his quiet voice soothed his tortured mind. I felt he had done his best to be kind and compassionate towards me, but his compassion held no warmth. It was so impersonal. I did not belong to Mother Church, and I had sinned too grievously to be accepted now. I had sinned against the fundamental solidarity of the family – the Holy Family of Mary and Joseph and the child Jesus – and the earthly family of mother, father and child, fashioned in the likeness of the other.

I had broken the Seventh Commandment.

In the cold, accusing eyes of the young priest, I was already condemned. He had done his duty as a good shepherd of the flock, for he had gathered a lost black sheep into the safe fold of Mother Church where he truly belonged by birthright. He was the youngest of the three priests at this church, scarcely more than a boy, and it must have been quite an ordeal for him, for Youth is so critical of Age.

Paul had asked me to spread a clean, white table napkin over the bedside table, and then to leave them together. I had done exactly as he wished. But when I opened the door to admit Father O'Brien, and the grave, boyish face confronted me, I was choked with tears, and lost for words. But he hardly noticed my distress, for his eyes had travelled quickly to the bed under the window, and the waxen face on the pillow.

I closed the door quietly, and locked myself in the lavatory, for there was no other place to hide.

Now I felt this grave young priest despised me for attending the funeral service. Perhaps, in his ardent adoration of the Holy Family, he imagined it to be a mockery. But who was mocked?

I sank to my knees and covered my stricken face with my hands, for the shining light of the candles blinded me with its brilliance. With my eyes closed I felt nearer to Paul, but I was so tired, and the voice of the priest was toneless and monotonous. When I opened my eyes again, the hunched figure of the old priest was standing at the foot of the coffin. He, too, had no substance. He, and the boy acolytes, with their candles, seemed to be acting in a play. And who were all these black-clothed figures kneeling in the pews? In sixteen years I had never once met them face to face. Today, for the first and last time, I was compelled to do so, for soon they would rise from their knees and move towards the centre aisle, to take their rightful place behind the bier - Paul's wife, Jacqueline, his adored daughter, Rosalinde, elderly sisters and their husbands who had flown over from America, and the rest would be business associates of pre-war years. All were there, Paul's people. We had kept our love apart, and tried to spare them embarrassment.

That compelling urge to be together was born of a chance meeting in May, 1942 - but love was so strong, it had survived the war years, unemployment, poverty, and Paul's prolonged illness. Paul had three distinct little worlds, and kept them apart - one for his work, one for his daughter, one for me. He enjoyed the company of men, good food and wine, and more than anything he enjoyed an audience. He saw life clearly and objectively. Life was for living, and he was not afraid of Life.

Was he afraid of Death? I shall never know. It came slowly and painfully, yet we had no time to say farewell. Why did I cradle his lifeless body in my arms for several hours before the doctor came? – and who fetched the doctor? I cannot remember.

'He's sleeping, Doctor. My poor darling, he was so tired,' I told him.

'Yes, he is sleeping. Come with me, my dear. Paul will not need you any more,' he said gently.

I shook my head, numb with exhaustion. How could there ever come a time when Paul would not need me?

'Come with me, my dear,' the doctor insisted.

So I laid Paul's head on the pillow, tucked the blanket under his chin, kissed his closed eyes, and followed the doctor obediently out of the room.

I held in my trembling hands a small missal I had found in the pew, to follow the Mass. It was open at Page 352 – I read the fifth line of the first collect over and over again, and my head was bursting.

'Put him out of mind for ever.'

But he is my mind – my heart – my life! He is possessed of me, and I of him.

'Grant we pray Thee, Almighty God, that the soul of Thy servant, Paul, who has today departed from this world, may be cleansed by this Sacrifice, and being thus rid of his sins, may find both forgiveness and everlasting rest.'

Were they coming to the end of the Mass?

'Dear God in heaven, don't take him away – not yet – not yet!' I was pleading desperately with God, for the moment I dreaded was almost upon me, but the toneless voice went on relentlessly, to the Absolution.

Paul had explained patiently about the Absolution. It was a simple and natural explanation of one of the great differences in our religious faith. Simple, that is, to a Catholic, born of Catholic parents, reared in a Catholic environment. But to me it was not acceptable. My prayers and confessions must be made direct to God, not to a priest. My sins could only be forgiven by God, or condemned by God on the Day of Judgment. They were my responsibility, and I could not be relieved of the burden – but Paul could. With all my heart I hoped and prayed that he was not mistaken.

'May his soul, and the souls of all the faithful departed, through the mercy of God, rest in peace.'

My stiffened lips formed the word 'Amen' – while a blinding stab of pain closed my eyes. A million little hammers beat on the crown of my head, and I was shaking as with palsy. The sour aftermath of sickness still clung to the roof of my mouth, and the stale odour of sweat hung about my clothes. I was unwashed for two, or was it three days? When I last glanced in a mirror, I did not recognize the face of the ageing woman, with lank, grey hair – expressionless as a mask.

Nobody noticed me now. Nobody would care if I didn't wash, or comb my hair.

The chapter was closed.

Perhaps those sixteen years with Paul had existed only in my imagination? The searing pain over my eyes numbed my mind, and the little hammers went on beating – beating – beating. I could neither go back nor forward, for I was suspended in the present moment.

Only a flicker of life supported me now in this final epilogue, for my heart had died on the instant my lips touched his ice-cold brow – the day the family arrived to claim his body for burial. The gap between us was widening. It was true then, what the doctor said the day Paul died? *'He will not need you any more.'*

They had received him back into their midst – the Family, and the Church.

I no longer existed for anyone. I felt I was floating away on the soft cloud of incense hovering over the candle-lit bier. I could still reach out my hands and take the hands of my lost love. I could kiss his hollowed cheeks and shadowed eyes. I could breathe life into those thin grey lips. But no, it was too late. They were closing in, and I could not reach him.

Struggling to my feet, I waited to face them as they came towards me. I should look upon their faces, and they would look on mine, for the first and last time. I should never see them again after today. *The chapter was closed.*

I knew exactly what I had to do – when they had taken Paul

away. I could never face that desolate bed-sitting-room again, and I had no strength left to search for another lodging. I had paid the rent and the milkman, and now I was almost a pauper. I had in my purse a few shillings and pence, together with a grubby ten shilling note the kindly landlady had pressed into my hand to buy flowers. Her face was wet with tears, and she seemed surprised at my own composure. I kissed her cheek, and thanked her for her sympathy. Then she closed the door on me – another departing tenant. It was her life.

Those shadowy figures from out of the past were moving towards me now – slowly – slowly – their steps measured by the Deacon's, they followed the bier down the aisle. Paul's wife, Jacqueline, had her daughter on one side, and Richard, her future son-in-law, on the other. These three were much taller than I had imagined them from the snapshots I had seen. But I had expected his wife to be poised and composed. She was warmly wrapped in a fur coat with a matching hat. Her hair was fashionably styled, and she was still a handsome woman. The girl's young, sorrowing face had the sad wistfulness of a child. She was weeping quietly. Oh, if I could take her in my arms and comfort her! We had shared Paul since she was six years old. She might even forgive me the years I had robbed her of her birthright? She looked much younger than her twenty-two years, in a tailored coat and Juliet cap. The dark, compelling eyes, wet with tears, were so like Paul's. In that moment of passing, I saw the selfishness of our love most clearly in that one face. For Paul's sake I had tried to love this child, but I had failed miserably, for I was jealous of her strong hold on him, and the tender relationship of parent and child that I should never know.

'But it makes no difference to us. She is my child. You are my sweetheart, my wife,' he told me, once, with a puzzled frown.

But they did not glance in my direction as they passed. How was it possible they still did not recognize 'that other woman'? Was it because of my dowdy appearance? Perhaps they thought I was the cleaner, paused in my duties out of respect for the dead?

The three elderly women and men would be Paul's sisters and their husbands, who had flown over from America. But they passed by, with bowed heads, in slow procession, and out of the church.

Now I was alone. It was over. Faintly in the distance I heard the cars drive away.

Then I stumbled weakly towards the door, and emptied my purse into a box labelled 'Crusade of Rescue'. I had no use for the money now. My hands were clenched over two small, familiar objects – the crucifix Paul had received at his first Communion – and his shaving brush. It was all that remained of our life together.

As I turned to look back, for the last time, at this quiet sanctuary of the soul, I heard distinctly and clearly, with compelling directness, the glorious voice of Gigli, singing the aria from the third act of *Turandot* – 'Nessun Dorma' – None shall sleep. This was Paul's favourite aria. I went out through the open door, borne on the wings of that rich, triumphant voice.